BAOFENG RADIO HANDBOOK

The Guerrilla Prepper's Comm Line

Veteran Survival Techniques
for Staying Connected
When the World Goes Silent

TRILLIUM SAGE
PUBLISHING

TODD FOSTER

ISBN 978-1-958118-52-8

TABLE OF CONTENTS

INTRODUCTION

The sky was an ominous gunmetal gray that fateful afternoon. Dark clouds gathered like troops would assemble for battle, and the first distant rumbles of thunder echoed through the valley. I should've seen it coming. Heck, the weather reports had been shouting warnings for days. But when you're a stubborn off-gridder who prides himself on self-reliance, you tend to ignore such "trivial" things as basic meteorology.

That's when the deluge hit. A torrent of raindrops began pummeling the tin roof of my remote cabin. Trees swayed violently in winds that howled like angry wolves. Within minutes, the once calm creek dividing me from the nearest town transformed into turbulent rapids, leaving only a few scattered wooden planks as remnants of the bridge.

Cut off, stranded, supplies dwindling, no means to call for help. No cell signal for miles. I was flat out of luck. Reality hit me harder than the rain; all my years of prepping were about to be put to the ultimate test of survival. But I had one last trusted ally ready for action: a humble little Baofeng handheld radio. With a few clicks of that magic box, I reached first responders and fellow preppers ready to lend aid. My off-grid communication lifeline!

That life-changing storm is why I'm here sharing the *Baofeng Radio Handbook* with you; a comprehensive guide to perhaps the most versatile and cost-effective backup communication tool a prepper or off-gridder could ever need. When the grids go down and the world goes dark, you'll want this pocket radio as close as your battle rifle and bug-out bag. Here you'll learn how the easily programmable Baofeng lets you monitor channels and frequencies for everything from weather alerts to local traffic to longwave survival broadcasts. We'll explore setting up secure off-grid networks with other radios enabling private communications when cellular towers are down. You'll even discover valuable prepper tips, like utilizing the Baofeng as an emergency power failure alarm.

This handbook dives into technical details and real-world applications alike. Need to boost your range? We've got you covered with antenna hacks. Looking to save repeater frequencies for areas along your bug-out route? No problem, we'll show you memory profiling like a pro. From selecting the right model and accessories to legal considerations, it's all here. But perhaps most importantly, you'll walk away with the hard-earned wisdom of never being caught off guard. Failing to use a dependable backup communication plan properly can spin a manageable crisis into a life-or-death scenario.

So spare yourself future regrets. When everything falls apart, a simple $30 radio can be your only lifeline. Just ask me about that one dark and stormy night...

Let's tune in and level up your prepper radio game.

Chapter 1
Choosing a Baofeng Model

Choosing the right Baofeng model is about as critical as deciding on your primary battle rifle. Get it wrong, and you might as well be taking a Nerf blaster into a live firefight.

The sheer number of different Baofeng radio models out there is enough to make your head spin. Dual-band, tri-band, analog, digital, UV-5Rs, UV-82HPs; it's enough to drown a grown man. But before you get too overwhelmed and panic buy the first cheap Chinese model you see on Amazon, hear me out. Settling on the wrong radio is a rookie mistake that'll handcuff your off-grid comms capabilities from the get-go. Maybe you need a compact, robust unit built to survive abusive conditions and endless patrols. Or perhaps you prefer a desktop rig with more output wattage to boost your signal range. Some of you comm junkies might even opt for a fancy dual-receiver model that pulls double duty.

The point is that each Baofeng variant caters to different priorities and budgets. Fail to understand these nuances, and you'll end up with a radio that's either overpowered and unnecessarily expensive for your needs, or woefully underpowered, leading to disappointment when you need it most. That's why I'm taking you straight into the core specs and real-world strengths of Baofeng's diverse lineup. We're going to strip away the marketing jargon to find out which models truly work for specific prepper needs.

From VHF/UHF combos to tri-banders packed with GMRS/FRS frequencies—by the time we're done, you'll wield the knowledge to cut through the noise and settle on a solid radio foundation perfectly tailored for your individual comms requirements and mission-critical demands.

So quit throwing gear money around like a drunken sailor, and start thinking like a calculated Comms Operator ready to make an educated purchase.

Understanding the Different Baofeng Models

It's time to put on your operator cap and start thinking like a comms specialist ready for any contingency. We're going to dive deep into three of Baofeng's most popular and capable handheld radios: the UV-5R, BF-F8HP, and UV-82HP.

I'm not just going to regurgitate some sterile manufacturer specs. You're getting the raw, unfiltered truth about how these units actually perform. We're talking real-world impressions, pros and cons, and most importantly, which radio is right for your specific go-bag communications strategy.

UV-5R

Antenna ----------- On/Off Volume Knob

-------- Flashlight

--------- LCD

SK side key 1/CALL ---------- VFO / MR

-------- Speaker/Microphone

PTT key --------- Accessory jack

LED indicator

SK side key 2/MONI

-------- Band key

A/B Key

-------- Keypad

Battery pack

The UV-5R is Baofeng's most well-known and affordable offering. This dual-band handheld is a game-changer that hooks many preppers into the world of two-way radios.

It's so affordable at around 25 bucks that you can buy a few spares as backups and still spend less than some folks do on a weekly ammo resupply. But don't let the low price tag fool you. The UV-5R packs a surprising amount of functionality for its size. You've got a dual-band VHF/UHF transceiver capable of hitting those critical 2m ham and 70cm frequencies. The included antenna might be a little stubby for the maximum range, but it's replaceable. And with around 4 watts of transmitting power, it'll reach far enough for local comms or hitting regional repeaters on the move.

Where the UV-5R really shines, though, is programming flexibility. This thing can be an absolute frequency-hopping, multi-mode dynamo when paired with the free CHIRP software and computer cabling. All those preprogrammed GMRS/FRS/MURS channels your standard FRS walkie-only dreams of. And you can absolutely code it to also transmit on those taboo FM broadcast frequencies that keep the music pumping when the grid's down. The downside of the UV-5R's crowd-pleasing appeal? It's built like a Toyota Corolla; reliable and economical, sure, but not capable of shrugging off heavy abuse for years on end. Drop it one too many times on a rocky trail and that plastic housing is going to crack and grenade. The stock antenna is also prone to getting waylaid by overhead branches and debris. Not ideal for hard use in the field.

- Specifications:
  - Dual-band VHF/UHF transceiver (136-174MHz VHF, 400-520MHz UHF)
  - Frequency range: 65-108MHz (FM broadcast), 136-174MHz (VHF), 400-520MHz (UHF)
  - Transmitting power: 4 watts (adjustable)
  - Channel capacity: 128 channels
  - Battery capacity: 1800mAh (Li-ion rechargeable)
  - Antenna: Removable, SMA-Female connector
  - Dimensions: 110 x 58 x 32mm
  - Weight: Approximately 210g (including battery and antenna)
  - Display: LCD display with backlight
  - Modes: FM radio, Dual Watch, Dual Standby, VFO/Memory channels scan
  - Programming: Manual programming or via computer software (CHIRP compatible)
  - Accessories: Includes battery, charger, antenna, belt clip, wrist strap, and user manual

- **Additional Features and User Experience:**
  - **Weight and size:** Weighing 244 g / 8.62 oz with battery and protective cover, the Baofeng UV-5R fits comfortably in your palm, with a size equivalent to a digital camera.
  - **Quality feel:** Users often note the UV-5R's initial impression of being "heavy and well-built." The fit and finish are excellent, with buttons and knobs that feel solid and provide positive feedback, enhancing the overall user experience.
  - **Flashlight:** Equipped with an LED flashlight on top, the UV-5R features a dedicated button for continuous light or strobe functions.
  - **FM Radio:** The UV-5R allows you to listen to Broadcast Radio from 65 to 108 MHz, automatically muting when incoming transmissions are detected.
  - **Loud audio output:** With 1000 mW audio output power, the UV-5R can easily fill a room with sound, ensuring clear and audible communication, even in noisy environments.
  - **Alarm function:** The UV-5R includes an alarm feature with a flashing white light, siren, and automatic transmission on the last selected frequency.

- ○ **Display and dual watch:** The UV-5R's display includes standby/receive/transmit indicators in different colors, user-selectable for easy identification. It also supports dual watches, allowing users to monitor two frequencies simultaneously for enhanced situational awareness.

- ○ **External speaker microphone:** For added convenience, the UV-5R is compatible with an external speaker microphone.

- ○ **Power options:** Users can choose between Low (1W) and High (5W) power settings, with independent reviews confirming real-life performance close to specifications.

- ○ **Computer programmable:** The UV-5R is computer programmable via free software, offering customization options and ease of programming.

- ○ **Long battery life and cost:** The UV-5R boasts a standby time of over 2 days, with a full charge taking 4 hours and a half charge taking 2 hours. Considering its robust features and capabilities, the UV-5R's affordability (under 50 dollars) makes it a cost-effective choice.

BF-F8HP

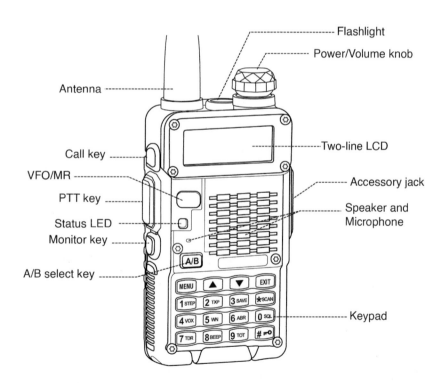

Think of the BF-F8HP as the radio equivalent of John McClane in *Die Hard*. It can take a beating, keep on ticking, and still sound crystal clear on 2m ham bands, all while enduring equal parts grime, explosions, and falling down air vents.

Built from a durable aluminum alloy that feels like it could double as a weapon, the BF-F8HP takes ruggedness to a completely new level for the Baofeng lineup. Waterproof to IPX7 specs and rated to military-grade impact resistance—this is the ideal comms gear for hard-charging preppers who never coddle their equipment. But the true beauty is under the hood; Baofeng pulled out all the stops with this one. You've got a high/low power toggle reaching up to 8 watts on the high end, and dual receive/dual watch capabilities that let you actively monitor two channels simultaneously. The expanded receive range spanning VHF/UHF plus FM broadcast frequencies adds serious versatility. And if you've ever dreamed of calling in fire support for an off-grid compound defense, the BF-F8HP's kill-switch direct frequency entry makes it a tactical dream.

The catch? You're paying a premium of around $60-70 for this type of tank-like construction and overbuilt engineering. For most preppers though, I'd argue the BF-F8HP hits that sweet spot of value and capability, ideal for rugged field communications.

- **Specifications:**
  - Dual-band VHF/UHF transceiver (136-174MHz VHF, 400-520MHz UHF)
  - Frequency range: 65-108MHz (FM broadcast), 136-174MHz (VHF), 400-520MHz (UHF)
  - Transmitting power: 8 watts (High)/ 4 watts (Medium)/ 1 watt (Low) (adjustable)
  - Channel capacity: 128 channels
  - Battery capacity: 2000mAh (Li-ion rechargeable)
  - Antenna: Removable, SMA-Female connector
  - Dimensions: 123 x 60 x 33mm
  - Weight: Approximately 250g (including battery and antenna)
  - Display: LCD display with backlight
  - Modes: FM radio, Dual Watch, Dual Standby, VFO/Memory channels scan
  - Programming: Manual programming or via computer software (CHIRP compatible)
  - Accessories: Includes battery, charger, antenna, belt clip, wrist strap, and user manual

- **Additional Features and User Experience:**
  - **Weight and size**: Weighing approximately 250g with battery and antenna, the BF-F8HP is slightly heavier and larger than the UV-5R, offering a more substantial feel in hand.
  - **Quality feel:** Users often describe the BF-F8HP as feeling well-built and sturdy, with buttons and knobs that provide tactile feedback.
  - **Flashlight:** Similar to the UV-5R, the BF-F8HP features an LED flashlight on top with a dedicated button for continuous light or strobe functions.

○ **FM radio:** The BF-F8HP allows you to listen to broadcast radio from 65 to 108 MHz, automatically muting when incoming transmissions are detected.

○ **Loud Audio Output**: With 1000 mW audio output power, the BF-F8HP delivers clear and loud audio, suitable for various environments.

○ **Alarm function:** The BF-F8HP includes an alarm feature with a flashing white light, siren, and automatic transmission on the last selected frequency.

○ **Display and dual watch:** The BF-F8HP's display includes standby/receive/transmit indicators in different colors, user-selectable for easy identification. It also supports a dual watch for monitoring two frequencies simultaneously.

○ **External speaker microphone:** Like the UV-5R, the BF-F8HP is compatible with an external speaker microphone for added convenience.

○ **Power options:** Users can select between High (8W), Medium (4W), and Low (1W) power settings, offering flexibility in transmission power based on needs and conditions.

○ **Long battery life and cost:** The BF-F8HP features a 2000mAh battery with a standby time of over 2 days. Charging time is approximately 4 hours for a full charge. The radio is priced competitively, offering value for its features and performance.

UV-82HP

Then, there's the new kid on the block - the UV-82HP. Baofeng clearly took notes from the success of the UV-5R and BF-F8HP when cooking up this tri-band beast of a handheld.

If the flexibility of 2m/70cm VHF/UHF bands still isn't quite enough for your multi-purpose comms needs, the UV-82 adds a third dedicated 1.25m band into the mix. That extra coverage unlocks a whole new world of NOAA weather channels, ham repeaters, plus some less legal "alternative" transmission methods. Unlike some earlier tri-banders plagued by frustrating VFOs for frequency adjustments, the UV-82HP packs in a straightforward keypad for direct entry punching. No more scrolling through banks for hours just to dial in a preprogrammed GMRS frequency listing. This little powerhouse also sports 5/8/4 watts of output for a true dual-PTT power toggle between high and low. Other features include:

- Cross-band half-duplex repeater capability for relaying signals when you're too far from the source.
- Dual receiver/dual monitoring to juggle multiple channels.
- A waterproof casing ready for the elements.
- A rock-solid magnesium alloy chassis that spits in the face of flimsy plastics.

If there's a catch to the UV-82 HP's impressive repertoire, it's the roughly $70 price tag. Not an outright deal breaker in my book for what you're getting. But if your budget is super tight, you could always opt for the venerable UV-5R and pick up an inexpensive second radio dedicated to that 1.25m range instead.

- **Specifications:**
    - Dual-band VHF/UHF transceiver (136-174MHz VHF, 400-520MHz UHF)
    - Frequency range: 65-108MHz (FM broadcast), 136-174MHz (VHF), 400-520MHz (UHF)
    - Transmitting power: 8 watts (High)/ 4 watts (Medium)/ 1 watt (Low) (adjustable)
    - Channel capacity: 128 channels
    - Battery capacity: 2000mAh (Li-ion rechargeable)
    - Antenna: Removable, SMA-Female connector
    - Dimensions: 123 x 60 x 33mm
    - Weight: Approximately 250g (including battery and antenna)
    - Display: LCD display with backlight
    - Modes: FM radio, Dual Watch, Dual Standby, VFO/Memory channels scan
    - Programming: Manual programming or via computer software (CHIRP compatible)
    - Accessories: Includes battery, charger, antenna, belt clip, wrist strap, and user manual

- **Additional Features and User Experience:**
  - **Weight and size:** Weighing approximately 250g with battery and antenna, the UV-82HP provides a substantial feel in hand, comparable to the BF-F8HP.

  - **Feel:** Users often describe the UV-82HP as feeling well-built and sturdy, with tactile buttons and knobs for ease of use.

  - **Flashlight:** Equipped with an LED flashlight on top, the UV-82HP offers continuous light or strobe functions for added versatility.

  - **FM radio:** Like other Baofeng models, the UV-82HP allows you to listen to broadcast radio from 65 to 108 MHz, automatically muting during transmissions.

  - **Loud audio output:** With 1000 mW audio output power, the UV-82HP delivers clear and loud audio suitable for various environments.

  - **Alarm function:** The UV-82HP includes an alarm feature with a flashing white light, siren, and automatic transmission on the last selected frequency for heightened alertness.

  - **Display and dual watch:** The UV-82HP's LCD display features standby/receive/transmit indicators in different colors, user-selectable for easy identification. It also supports a dual watch for monitoring two frequencies simultaneously.

  - **External speaker microphone:** Compatible with an external speaker microphone, the UV-82HP offers added convenience during use.

  - **Power options:** Users can select between High (8W), Medium (4W), and Low (1W) power settings, providing flexibility in transmission power based on needs and conditions.

  - **Long battery life and cost:** Featuring a 2000mAh battery, the UV-82HP offers over 2 days of standby time. Charging time is approximately 4 hours for a full charge, making it suitable for extended use. The radio's competitive pricing offers value for its features and performance.

At the end of the day, there's no such thing as a true "one size fits all" Baofeng model for every prepper and comms scenario. But now that you've got the raw intel on three of the brand's most popular offerings, you should be able to wade through the marketing hype and choose the radio that best fits your personal survival communications philosophy. So quit gambling on random Amazon purchases and do it right by outfitting your kit with the proper hardware from day one. Because when civilization grinds to a halt and the world turns into a real-life *Fallout* wasteland, the quality of your radio gear could mean the difference between mustering critical aid or getting lost in the static.

It's on you to properly kit up. Radio isolation is a death sentence in the off-grid world, so choose wisely.

Factors to Consider When Selecting the Right Model

Choosing the right Baofeng radio is about more than blindly grabbing the cheapest model.

It's a calculated decision that requires carefully evaluating your individual needs and mission-critical demands. Get it wrong, and you could be stuck with an ill-equipped piece of gear that becomes a glorified paperweight when you need it most. To help you avoid those rookie stumbles, I'm breaking down the key factors you absolutely must consider before locking in your Baofeng purchase.

- **Intended Use**
  - Are you an everyday ham radio enthusiast just looking for an affordable way to hit the 2m/70cm bands? Or is this strictly for off-grid survival communications?
  - Your intended use determines whether you need a barebones entry-level model for casual operation, or an overbuilt unit ready to handle extended, harsh prepper environments.

- **Frequency Range**
  - Baofeng offers radios covering VHF, UHF, and even tri-band models hitting the 1.25m range. But what bands do you need based on your area's regulations and repeater networks?
  - Do your due diligence to avoid wasting money on frequencies you can't legally transmit without a license. You don't want an FCC (Federal Communications Commission) violation on top of everything else when society collapses.

- **Durability and Build Quality**
  - Let's be real—not every prepper needs a radio encased in an aluminum-magnesium alloy designed to survive nuclear Armageddon. Sometimes that extra ruggedness just adds unnecessary cost and weight.
  - But if you plan on hauling gear through the backcountry or relying on this radio as long-term backup, you'd better invest in a hard-use model that can shrug off drops, water intrusion, and general field abuse.

- **Battery Life**
  - In an ideal world, we'd all have radios with infinite power that never require new batteries. But when operating off-grid with limited charging sources, long-term battery endurance is critical.
  - Consider models with power-saving features, battery life indicators, and compatibility with extended-life batteries. Changing those small components every day becomes tiresome quickly.

- **Size and Portability**
  - You can opt for a compact pocket-sized handheld for everyday carry convenience. But that tiny form factor often comes at the expense of reduced output wattage, stubby antennas, and limited range.
  - If punching long-distance signals is a priority, you may need to bite the bulk bullet for a larger mobile rig...even if that sacrifices some portability.

- **Antenna Compatibility**
  - Some Baofeng radios may offer compatibility with external antennas, allowing you to enhance signal strength and range.
  - Consider this if you expect to need extended coverage in certain environments.

- **Water Resistance**
  - While not all Baofeng models are waterproof, some may offer varying degrees of water resistance.
  - If you expect to use the radio in wet or rainy conditions, prioritize models with water-resistant features to ensure durability and functionality.

- **Display Visibility**
  - Evaluate the visibility and clarity of the LCD display, especially in varying lighting conditions. A clear and bright display with adjustable backlighting can enhance usability during nighttime or low-light operations.

- **User Interface**
  - Consider the user interface design and ease of navigation. Intuitive controls and a straightforward menu structure can simplify operation, especially for users with limited radio experience or in high-stress situations.

- **Compatibility with Accessories**
  - Check compatibility with accessories such as headsets, microphones, and external speakers.

- Having the option to use compatible accessories can improve comfort, convenience, and communication effectiveness.

- **Legal Compliance**
  - Ensure that the radio model complies with local regulations and licensing requirements for transmitting on specific frequencies.

  - Unlicensed transmission on restricted frequencies can lead to legal issues and penalties.

- **Software and Firmware Updates**
  - Check if the radio supports software and firmware updates.

  - Regular updates can enhance performance, add new features, and address any bugs or issues, ensuring long-term usability and functionality.

- **Warranty and Support**
  - Consider the warranty period and customer support services.

  - A reliable warranty and responsive customer support can provide peace of mind and assistance in case of any technical issues or concerns.

- **Additional Features**
  - From dual PTT power levels to dual watch and cross-band repeat capabilities—Baofeng packs a lot of useful bells and whistles into its lineup. But which ones do you need?

  - If it's truly just a basic backup comms device, you can skip the pricier tri-band models or digital capabilities. But power output, programming flexibility, and multi-mode operation are essential for primary radios.

There's no one-size-fits-all "best" Baofeng model out there. It comes down to understanding your personal requirements and finding the right balance of features, frequencies, durability, and affordability that perfectly fits your survival communications strategy. Take a hard look at your local conditions, budget limitations, and comms philosophy before letting me recommend specific models. Half the prepper radios collecting dust in buddies' go-bags result from buying the wrong tool for the job.

Don't be that guy staring blankly at a useless radio when lives are on the line and you need to call for backup. Do your diligence from the start and grab the properly equipped hardware.

Budget-Friendly Options Versus Feature-Rich Models

There's no such thing as a free lunch in this hobby. Do you want cutting-edge features and performance? Be prepared to open up that war wallet.

But that doesn't mean the budget-constrained among us are completely out of luck either. Baofeng has built its reputation on offering solid entry-level radios that punch well above their bargain-basement price tags in terms of capability. The key is understanding what you're giving up at each different price tier so you can make an educated decision.

Let's explore the two ends of the Baofeng spectrum:

- **Budget Blasters: The Sub-$50 Offerings**
  - Models like the legendary UV-5R and UV-82C fall into this rock-bottom category—cheap as hell, yet still semi-capable.

- You're obviously not getting the tank-like build quality of the premium models. Flimsy plastic housing, questionable waterproofing, short antenna ranges...it's very much a grab-and-go disposable unit.

- But for basic local VHF/UHF comms, these budget blasters can still hit the 2m/70cm bands well enough for close-range ops or keying up a repeater. Just don't expect miracles for distance or durability.

- No, they're nowhere near true top-shelf handheld performance. But a $25 UV-5R is one helluva backup option that gives you basic ham coverage on a beer budget.

- **The Prime Cut: Premium $60-$100 Radios**
    - We're talking about models like the BF-F8HP and UV-9R on the premium end of the Baofeng scale. Serious hardware for serious preppers not messing around.

    - Build quality takes a major leap with over-engineered aluminum alloy chassis, better water/dust sealing, and a thick mil-spec design that can legitimately shrug off abuse for years.

    - Expect maximum legal power transmission over dual/tri-band operation covering everything from GMRS (General Mobile Radio Service) to NOAA (National Oceanic and Atmospheric Administration) weather. These are true base units masquerading as handhelds.

    - Extended battery life features, heat sinks for high output, even luxuries like a dual watch, cross-band repeat, and scanning...the whole nine yards of features tailored for field communications.

    - The downside? Spending upwards of $70-100 pushes the limits of what some would call a "budget" prepper radio purchase. If money is tight, some of these premium specs border on overkill.

So how do you determine whether it's worth saddling up for a premium model versus just grabbing an affordable base unit? It all comes down to prioritizing your precise needs and budget constraints:

- **Local Comms and Light Use?**
    - If you're a weekend prepper who just needs to hit the local repeaters for some neighborhood watch updates, a basic $25 entry model should cover your bases.

    - The same applies if this is purely an emergency backup radio riding in your vehicle or go-bag as a just-in-case contingency for a local grid-down scenario. It's better than being totally dark.

- **Hard Off-Grid Field Use For Extended Periods?**
  - Now, if you're envisioning roving patrols, bug-out contingencies, and operating as a mobile survivalist unit, those cheap budget options may show their limitations quickly.

  - Limited power output means reduced range. Short battery life is a liability on multi-day ops. And good luck if you drop one of those flimsy units from any kind of height—it'll shatter like a porcelain doll.

  - In this case, the heavy-duty aluminum/polycarbonate construction and extended feature set of a premium $70-100 model is worth the investment to ensure reliable long-haul comms.

- **Licensed Ham Seeking SHTF Versatility?**
  - For licensed amateur radio operators looking to take advantage of the maximum legal frequencies and power available, premium radios unlock way more flexibility for improvised disaster preparedness.

  - GMRS frequencies, NOAA weather channels, and cross-band repeater; these advanced functions give you way more survival bandwidth versus a basic budget unit.

  - It's not a must for newbies without a license, but seasoned radio enthusiasts serious about their emergency gear won't want to skip this one.

Be brutally honest about your experience level, intended applications, and how much cash you can responsibly funnel into this kit. Myself? I'd never rely solely on those bare-bones budget units for any type of prolonged field ops. Too many compromises on range, output, and durability that could leave you stranded when you need solid comms. But I'm also not made of money, so I look for underrated premium gems that squeeze maximum features and performance in that $60-80 sweet spot. That's why models like the BF-F8HP are my preferred go-to. You get the heavy-duty construction to shrug off a war zone's worth of abuse while still packing unreal flexibility with dual-watch, high/low power output, cross-band functionality; pretty much every mission-critical bell and whistle you could ask for in a prepper radio at a sub-$100 price point. But I've also got a couple of cheap Baofeng HT walkies stashed in vehicles and bunkers just for short-range contingency use. It's all about adapting your grasp of these radios' pros, cons, and niche strengths to your specific survival philosophy and resource constraints.

So stop guessing, stop indiscriminately throwing dollars around, and figure out the smart move. Fail to plan your comms for reality, and you're just planning to get comms failures—plain and simple. Speaking of plain and simple, let's radio in on some basic operations.

Chapter 2
Unboxing and Basic Operations

The excitement of unboxing your new Baofeng radio after all your research is unbeatable. You've analyzed the specs, weighed the costs, and pulled the trigger on the model best suited for your off-grid communications needs.

Hold off on unboxing just yet; not learning the basics first can lead to confusion, misuse, and legal trouble. You need to start strong and unbox your radio like a seasoned pro. We're getting into the nuanced steps required to safely power up, tune frequencies, and manipulate fundamental settings on your specific Baofeng model.

From meticulous battery installations to programming those first critical channels, you'll receive a guided tour covering every essential task needed to transition your new radio from dormant Chinese import to active-duty field communications unit ready for action. And don't even think about half-assing this process with the mentality of "I'll just figure it out later." Incorrect setup leads to premature wear and tear, programming mishaps violating local transmission laws, or even damaging your new radio. Real communication specialists don't fumble with those entry-level tasks.

Let's get to work.

Step-by-Step Guide to Unboxing Your Baofeng Radio

The unboxing process for any new radio gear isn't something to be taken lightly. One missed step and you could be staring at a scrambled mess of uninstalled antennas, mishandled batteries, and critical accessory pieces strewn about.

This is a meticulous procedure to be executed with focus and precision. Deviate from the plan at your own risk of crippling your new radio before it ever hits the airwaves. If you've got your Baofeng shipment sitting pretty, pay attention. I'm running you through the full unboxing session, component by component, leaving no room for guesswork or error.

- **Outer Packaging**
  - Don't be an impatient savage ripping into that box like a Christmas present. Carefully slice the packing tape and outer cardboard shell to preserve it as a safe storage vessel.

  - Once opened, perform a quick visual inventory matching the inner contents against the shipping inventory list, if provided. Are numbers not adding up? Initiate a return before proceeding.

- **The Radio Itself**
  - With the system unit safely removed from its cardboard cocoon, take a preliminary look for any obvious signs of shipping damage: cracks, dents, scratches, etc. Document any issues.

  - Do not power it on yet. Serious rookie mistake before ensuring proper battery installation and attaching the antenna.

  - Speaking of which, delicately set the radio aside on an approved anti-static mat or surface while you gear up the remaining components.

- **Battery Handling**
  - Whether it comes with a rechargeable Li-ion battery pack or a traditional AA battery caddy, proper battery handling is crucial to avoid premature wear or dangerous mishaps.
  - With rechargeables, inspect for any dents or damage and ensure charge levels are topped off from the factory using the included charger before installation.
  - For AA types, always opt for premium brand names over discount bin bargains which can leak corrosive gunk prematurely.
  - Either way, read the manual section covering proper battery installation and polarity orientation. Forcing them backward is a good way to kiss that fancy new radio goodbye.

- **Antennas & Cabling**
  - Most Baofeng handhelds will include a rigid stock antenna, but its short rigid length means disappointing range. Carefully unpack any upgraded antenna options and set them aside.
  - For mobile unit installs, locate the battery cabling for direct power supply hookups, any antenna mounting hardware, and cabling accouterments. Organization is key.
  - If an upgraded antenna was also purchased, triple-check the connector types to ensure compatibility before attempting installation. Cross-threading those connections is a painfully easy way to ruin both pieces.

- **Manuals & Documentation**
  - Probably the least-valued component in the box, but responsible operators know the cardinal sin of chucking the manuals and reference documentation before reading them thoroughly.
  - These guides contain critical info on proper setup procedures, troubleshooting techniques, legal requirements around frequency usage, and FCC transmission rules to avoid violations.
  - At a minimum, skim the included manuals and make note of important chapters to reference when tackling configuration and first-usage steps later on.

- **External Accessories**
  - Finally, inspect any additional accessories included with the unit—charging docks, lapel mics, earpieces, carrying cases, and the like. Make sure quantities match the packing slip.
  - My recommendation? Store them safely packaged up until actually needed to avoid premature loss or damage during initial radio configuration and testing.

With the core unboxing components now accounted for, organized, and preliminarily inspected for any shipping issues, you've checked the first critical box to ensure a smooth transition into active radio operations. But you're not out of the woods yet. Without taking the proper first-usage precautions like installing antennas and batteries per manufacturer specs, you risk prematurely damaging or mishandling critical components before that new gear ever hits the field. Stick to the plan. Display some discipline and attention to detail to reap the rewards later without the rookie pitfalls. Anything less disrespects the gear you just invested premium dollars into acquiring.

A radio that's misconfigured or missing an antenna is the kind of amateur incompetence that turns you into a punchline faster than you can transmit "What's your twenty?"

Basic Setup and Initial Configuration

Your new Baofeng radio emerged unscathed and accounted for. But we're not across the finish line just yet.

The path to getting that new unit properly set up and initially configured for field duty is a detail-oriented minefield littered with potential pitfalls. Miss a single step in this crucial setup phase, and you're staring down the barrel of premature equipment damage, improper frequency programming, or even disastrous battery mishaps. From this point forward, you turn those radios into an extension of your own body, handling them with the same care and precision. Anything less is just a risk.

- **Battery Installation**
  - Whether using rechargeable battery packs or standard disposables, proper battery installation is Radio Care 101.

  - First, consult the manual illustrations to orient the batteries for proper polarity, installing them backward is a hotline straight to the radio room inferno.

  - Rechargeables get seated securely and clicked into place. Disposable caddies receive fresh premium batteries, not those discount bin crisis leakers.

  - Once installed, do a press test by attempting to power on briefly to confirm connection integrity. Are red lights flashing? Try reseating the pack from scratch.

- **Antenna Attachment**
  - Your new Baofeng likely came bundled with a short-stock antenna suited for basic local operation. But we're aiming bigger than that.

  - Any upgraded antennas get connected by carefully spinning the threaded base onto the radio's antenna port. Gentle yet firm quarter-turn spins are key to avoiding cross-threading.

  - But don't be tempted to over-tighten and crank that sucker down with a gorilla's grip either. That would strip out the entire antenna mount.

  - Once sufficiently snug, do not attempt to bend or snap the antenna into a compact position until after verifying the radio function.

  - When installing external antennas or mobile units, ensure proper alignment and grounding. Improper antenna installation can lead to signal loss, interference, or damage to the radio.

- **Battery Charging**
  - Rechargeable battery packs coming from the factory floor should have a small reserve charge, but topping them off is SOP (Standard Operating Procedure) to ensure maximum operational time.

  - Use only the included "dumb" charging cradle or recommended power supply intended for your specific lithium battery chemistry. Improvising is asking for a thermal event.

  - For disposables, no charging is required, but keep those premium sealed packs loaded up and ready to hot-swap in the field if the primary set drains.

- ○ Develop smart power management habits now by routinely recharging any spare or drained packs immediately.

- **Powering On**
  - ○ With batteries installed, antennas mounted, and power reserves topped off, it's finally time to put that new Baofeng through its initial paces.

  - ○ For handhelds, the power button is usually on the left side or top edge. Press and hold until the welcome screen or LED activation lights initialize.

  - ○ Mobile and desktop rigs add an extra power supply cable from the battery that must be plugged into the DC jack before powering up the head unit.

  - ○ Whether via software or physical button, turn OFF any noise blanker, scrambler, or encoding features that could interfere with basic output.

  - ○ In radio menu settings, temporarily block all channels and set them to a clear frequency to avoid transmitting during these first power-on tests. More on active rx ("receive" in radio terminology) later.

With the foundational hardware components now properly installed and sufficient battery reserves, your fresh new Baofeng is now officially awakened from its factory slumber. But we're still operating in a carefully controlled test environment to avoid any accidental broadcasts or dangerous power malfunctions. Rookie mistakes breed bad habits, and the last thing any of us needs in an off-grid situation is a bunch of undisciplined operators broadcasting over open frequencies.

Lock in these basic procedures like the back of your hand.

Familiarizing Yourself with the Buttons and Functions

Fundamental interface mastery isn't some eccentric prepper delicacy; it's an absolute necessity for any self-respecting off-grid operator aiming to wield their gear with true authority.

Do you think getting caught flat-footed and unable to manipulate basic volume levels or channel selection is going to do you any favors when you're scanning for that critical emergency broadcast? Or fumbling around like an amateur when you need to squash the squelch on a distant repeater signal? It's just going to land you and your team in hot water by getting outflanked and overwhelmed.

That's why you'll master the button layouts, interface navigation, and display interpretation until you can operate your Baofeng radio with ease and precision.

We're excising those gray areas of uncertainty to establish clearly defined areas of mastery. Let's get started:

- **Button Layouts**
  - Regardless of the model, every Baofeng has some variation of the power button, PTT (Push-to-Talk) switch, volume/squelch knob, VFO (Variable Frequency Oscillator) selector, and 4-way directional navigation pad.

    - **Power button:** Usually located on the top or side of the radio, often marked with a power symbol (⏻).

    - **PTT (Push-to-Talk) switch:** Typically found on the side of the radio, easily accessible by the thumb or index finger when holding the radio.

    - **Volume/squelch knob:** Positioned on the top or front of the radio, sometimes combined into a single knob for volume control and squelch adjustment.

    - **VFO (Variable Frequency Oscillator) selector:** Usually labeled as "VFO/MR" and located near the volume knob or as a dedicated button on the front panel.

    - **4-Way directional navigation pad:** Located on the front panel, consisting of up, down, left, and right arrows for menu navigation and selection.
  - More premium setups add programmable auxiliary buttons, dual channel knobs for A/B splits, and supplemental menu buttons. But we're focused on sharpening that base skillset first.
  - From power up to basic ops, grip that unit and commit the physical locations of each primary control interface to memory.
  - Take note of any additional buttons or knobs specific to your Baofeng model and learn their functions. This may include emergency buttons, memory recall buttons, or scan options.

- **Basic Function Familiarity**
  - Beyond just locating buttons, you'd better internalize exactly which ones dictate functions like changing VFO/channel banks, finessing volume/squelch levels, and activating keypad locks.

    - Power button turns the radio on/off
    - PTT switch initiates transmissions
    - Volume/squelch knob adjusts audio output and filters noise
    - VFO selector switches between frequency modes, and the navigation pad navigates menus and settings.
  - Internalize the specific actions associated with each button press, toggle, or twist to perform core operations on your Baofeng radio:

- **Power Button:**
  - Press and hold to power on/off the radio.
  - Short press to toggle between standby and active modes.

- **PTT (Push-To-Talk) Button:**
  - Press and hold while speaking to transmit your message.
  - Release to listen to incoming transmissions.

- **Volume/Squelch Knob:**
  - Twist clockwise to increase volume.
  - Twist counterclockwise to decrease volume.
  - Adjust squelch settings to filter out background noise.

- **VFO Selector:**
  - Toggle between VFO (Variable Frequency Oscillator) and memory channel modes.
  - Use to select different frequency bands or channels.

- **Directional Navigation Pad:**
  - Up/Down: Navigate through menu options or scroll frequency/channel lists.
  - Left/Right: Adjust settings or switch between menu functions.
  - Center/Enter: Confirm selections or access sub-menus.

- **Programmable Auxiliary Buttons (if available):**
  - Customize these buttons for quick access to frequently used features or functions.
  - Assign functions like scanning, emergency alerts, or direct channel selection.

- **Dual Channel Knobs (if available):**
  - Used to adjust settings for two different channels simultaneously in A/B split mode.
  - Convenient for monitoring or switching between two frequencies quickly.

- **Supplemental Menu Buttons:**
  - Access additional menu options or settings not available directly through the main controls.
  - Used to configure advanced features, set radio parameters, or program custom settings.

- **Keypad Lock Activation:**
  - Press and hold a designated button or combination to lock/unlock the keypad.
  - Prevents accidental button presses or settings changes during operation.

- **Direct Frequency/Channel Entry:**
  - Enter specific frequencies or channel numbers directly using the keypad.
  - Allows for quick tuning to desired frequencies without scrolling through lists.

- **Function Buttons (such as A/B, FM, and Monitor):**
  - Activate specific functions like toggling between A/B channels, switching to FM radio mode, or monitoring activity on a channel.

- Avoid getting lost in nested sub-menu layers by mastering shortcuts or direct access methods for common tasks like channel swapping and frequency adjustments. Mastering these shortcuts and direct access methods will streamline common tasks:

  - **Channel Swapping:**
    - Use the "A/B" button to toggle between two saved channels.
    - Press the numeric keypad followed by "Enter" for direct access to a specific channel.

  - **Keypad Lock/Unlock:**
    - Press and hold the "Lock" or "Func" button to lock/unlock the keypad to prevent accidental button presses.

  - **Frequency Adjustments:**
    - Use the VFO/MR (Variable Frequency Oscillator/Memory Recall) button to switch between frequency input and memory recall modes.
    - Enter the desired frequency directly using the numeric keypad, followed by "Enter" to confirm.

  - **Direct Frequency Input:**
    - Press the "VFO/MR" button to enter frequency input mode directly, allowing you to input the desired frequency using the numeric keypad.

  - **Memory Channel Recall:**
    - Press the "VFO/MR" button to switch to memory recall mode and use the numeric keypad to select a stored memory channel.

  - **Volume Control:**
    - Twist the volume knob to adjust the audio output level.

- Press the "Func" button followed by the volume knob to quickly mute/unmute the audio.

- **Squelch Adjustment:**
  - Use the "Func" button in combination with the volume knob to adjust the squelch level for better signal reception.

- **Scan Mode Activation:**
  - Press the "Scan" button to initiate scanning mode, which automatically searches for active channels or frequencies.

- **Emergency Alerts:**
  - Assign an auxiliary button for emergency alerts or quick access to predefined emergency frequencies.

- **Monitor Mode:**
  - Use the "Monitor" button to temporarily disable the squelch and listen for weak or distant signals.

- Practice using the radio's basic functions regularly to maintain proficiency and prevent fumbling during critical communications.

- Refer to the user manual for detailed instructions on using each function and customizing settings to optimize performance.

- Explore advanced features gradually once you have a solid understanding of the basic functions, avoiding unnecessary complexity until you're comfortable with core operations.

- Regularly review and reinforce your knowledge of basic functions to ensure the smooth and reliable operation of your Baofeng radio.

- **LCD Interpretation**
  - With physical interface locations and mapped functions on lockdown, it's time to interpret the information being projected.

  - Power levels, battery life indicators, frequency dig readouts, channel banks, PL/DPL codes, and encryption modes, you'd better be able to rattle off the meaning of every HUD symbol.

    - **Battery icon:** Indicates the remaining battery charge level. A full battery icon means the battery is fully charged, while a low battery icon indicates a need for recharging.

- **Antenna icon:** Shows the status of the antenna connection. A solid antenna icon means the antenna is connected properly, while a flashing or missing antenna icon indicates an issue with the antenna connection.

- **Transmitting icon:** This appears when the radio is transmitting a signal. It may be a microphone symbol or an arrow pointing upwards.

- **Signal strength icon:** Displays the signal strength of the received signal. More bars indicate a stronger signal, while fewer bars suggest a weaker signal.

- **Receiving icon:** Indicates that the radio is receiving a signal. It may be a speaker symbol or an arrow pointing downwards.

- **Scan icon:** This appears when the radio is scanning through channels or frequencies. It may be an arrow moving across channels or a rotating symbol.

- **Frequency display:** Shows the current frequency the radio is tuned to, usually in MHz (megahertz).

- **Mode indicator:** Indicates the operating mode of the radio, such as FM (Frequency Modulation), AM (Amplitude Modulation), or other modes.

- **Channel number/name:** Displays the current channel number or name that the radio is tuned to.

- **Keypad lock icon:** Appears when the keypad lock function is activated, preventing accidental button presses.

- **Menu indicator:** Indicates that the radio is in the menu mode, allowing you to access and configure settings.

- **Volume level indicator:** Shows the current volume level of the radio's speaker or headset.

- **Memory channel indicator:** This shows when the radio is using a memory channel for saved frequencies or settings.

- **Dual watch icon:** Appears when the radio is in dual watch mode, monitoring two frequencies simultaneously.

- **Dual standby icon:** Indicates dual standby mode, where the radio is ready to receive on two frequencies but can only transmit one at a time.

- **Squelch level indicator:** Displays the squelch level setting, which controls background noise and interference.

- **CTCSS/DCS indicator:** Indicates when CTCSS (Continuous Tone-Coded Squelch System) or DCS (Digital-Coded Squelch) is enabled for selective calling or privacy codes.

- **VOX (Voice Operated Transmit) indicator:** Appears when VOX mode is activated, allowing hands-free operation based on voice activation.

- **Busy channel indicator:** Alerts you when a channel is busy and cannot be used for transmission.

- **Clock/time display:** Shows the current time if the radio has a built-in clock or timer feature.

- **Timer indicator:** Displays timers for functions like timeout timer, scan delay, or other time-based settings.

- **Alert indicator:** Indicates alerts such as low battery, channel busy, or other system notifications.

- **FM radio mode indicator:** Appears when the radio is in FM radio mode, allowing you to listen to broadcast radio stations.

○ That digital dashboard is feeding you a constant operational snapshot when executing field comms. Any gaps in decoding those visual feeds could prove disastrous.

This table provides a clearer description of each button/command, its appearance, and where it's typically located:

FUNCTION	BUTTON/COMMAND	DESCRIPTION/LOCATION
Power On/Off	Power Button	Typically a circular button on the top or side
Channel Up	Up Arrow	Upward arrow symbol on the keypad or side button
Channel Down	Down Arrow	Downward arrow symbol on the keypad or side button
Volume Up	Volume Up Button	Upward arrow or "+" symbol on the keypad or side
Volume Down	Volume Down Button	Downward arrow or "-" symbol on the keypad or side
Menu	Menu Button	Labeled "Menu" or "Menu/Exit" on the keypad or side
Select	Select Button	"Select" or "Enter" labeled button on the keypad
Monitor (Open Squelch)	Moni Button	The "Moni" or "Monitor" button is often labeled as such
Lock/Unlock Keypad	Lock Button	"Lock" or "Key Lock" button to lock/unlock keys
Scan Channels	Scan Button	The "Scan" button for scanning available channels
Dual Watch	Dual Watch Button	"DW" or "Dual" button for dual watch mode
Voice Prompt	Voice Button	The button labeled "Voice" or for the voice prompt
Side Key Programming	Side Keys	Buttons on the side, programmable for shortcuts
Emergency Alarm	Alarm Button	"Alarm" button for emergency alarm activation
Transmit (PTT)	PTT Button	"PTT" or "Push to Talk" button for transmitting
Mode Switch	Mode Button	"Mode" button for switching between modes

FUNCTION	BUTTON/COMMAND	DESCRIPTION/LOCATION
Keypad	Keypad Buttons	Numeric keypad for frequency input and settings
Function Keys	FN Keys	Function keys for accessing secondary functions
LED Flashlight	Flashlight Button	Button for activating the built-in LED flashlight
Backlight	Backlight Button	Button to turn on/off the backlight display
Battery Saver	BCL Button	"BCL" or "Battery Saver" button for power saving
Tone Squelch	TSQL Button	"TSQL" or "Tone" button for tone squelch
CTCSS/DCS	CTDCS Button	"CTCSS" or "DCS" button for CTCSS/DCS settings
Shift (Frequency)	Shift Button	"Shift" button for frequency shift adjustments
Repeater	Repeater Button	"Repeater" button for repeater mode operations
Memory Channels	MR Button	"MR" or "Memory" button for memory channel access
Frequency Input	Frequency Keypad	Keypad for entering frequency and settings

The path to true Baofeng mastery doesn't stop at just handling the hardware and operating system menus. Genuine expertise demands hardcore shorthand familiarization with every aspect of the HUD (Heads-Up Display) to maintain ruthless situational awareness out there. Can you spot an incorrect frequency projection or encryption mismatch at a glance? Diagnose a signal reception issue by cross-checking the display codes? Interpret what's happening and make snap corrections without spraying the place with questions first? That's the level of enlightened radio symbiosis I'm talking about. Baofeng's LCDs, buttons, and codecs have to become a literal extension of your central nervous system as a modern comms operator.

It starts with grinding out these elementary functions and displaying interpretations until they're baked into your DNA. If you don't want to end up in trouble when things get serious, you've got to master your radio skills like a pro. Panicking and fumbling with settings won't cut it when danger strikes. So, take the time to learn the basics inside out and commit them to memory.

Chapter 3
Radio Terminology and Communications

We've spent plenty of time on the whole nine yards of "Radio Basics 101." But beneath that seemingly straightforward machinery lies an entire world of standardized terminology, protocols, and fundamental operating principles that keep the organized radio bands from devolving into a squawking wasteland.

Unless you want your Baofeng privileges revoked, you'd better internalize the conceptual framework behind proper communication etiquette. This is your formal induction into the "cult" of codified radio lingo—a no-hazing primer that breaks down all the core concepts and unspoken rules in plain language. No more getting lost in the woods whenever someone radios on about PL tones, repeater outputs, or the importance of contextualizing your vocals. From dissecting FCC (the regulatory authority and oversight provided by the Federal Communications Commission) governance and legal frequency allocations to nailing the fundamentals of clear voice discipline.

Roger that? You should be able to hold your own in any op brief without involuntary eye twitches.

Mastering this domain of terminology and communications theory isn't just some IQ rationalization exercise. It's the only path to unlocking your Baofeng's full potential as an extended survival tool. Skipping these steps in favor of slapping that radio onto a random open freq and barking out unplanned comms is amateur bushcraft that'll get you blackballed from survival circles. Mastering radio communication means knowing why you organize the airwaves so precisely.

So settle in, get that mental notebook ready, and prepare to download some real operating foundational wisdom. We're raising the standards, not chasing shortcuts.

An Introduction to Essential Radio Terminology

This lingo isn't just pedantic technobabble, it's the coded language of the radio waves you'll need fluent mastery over to navigate the chaos. So absorb these core vocabulary lessons.

Let's lay out the academic framework to support your comms:

- **Frequency**
  - The primordial atomic element upon which all radio communications are built. Frequency refers to those cyclical sine waves measured in Hertz.

  - Higher frequencies like UHF enable tighter signal concentrations over shorter ranges. Lower VHF broadcast is wilder but can penetrate walls and vegetation better.

  - Bottom line: understanding frequency behaviors and allocations is key to tailoring your Baofeng for optimal coverage and regulatory compliance in the field.

- **Channels**
  - Rather than comms being a lawless free-for-all, available frequencies get divided into organized channel groupings to prevent airwave Armageddon.

  - Designated channel banks exist for everything from FRS blasters to GMRS freqs, MURS, ham, NOAA weather, and the works. Straying into unauthorized zones is a serious no-go.

- o Proper channel programming and allocations keep transmissions segregated between intended recipient groups and licensed operations. Do it wrong and catch hell.

- **Modulation**
  - o At its core, modulation refers to the act of superimposing or encoding raw data signals onto those carrier radio frequencies as a transmission medium.
  - o Amplitude Modulation (AM) and Frequency Modulation (FM) are the classics, but more advanced modes like QAM (Quadrature Amplitude Modulation) handle heavy bandwidth broadband data-casting.
  - o The modulation protocol you run determines encoding fidelity and resilience to interference or noise on congested frequencies in the field. Critical stuff.

- **Transceivers**
  - o Unlike standard broadcast units, transceivers like your Baofeng are dual-threat devices combining both transmission and reception capabilities.
  - o They don't just blast signals, they constantly monitor incoming frequencies and automatically retransmit relevant traffic across the network.
  - o Mastering the send/receive functionality is very important because even in crisis survival situations, occupying an open channel with mindless one-way chatter helps no one.

That's just a tiny sample platter of the lingo benchmarks you'll need to raise your radio game. There's plenty more where that came from too—safety/service tone codes, escalation procedures, repeater protocols, interference mitigation, you name it.

The following summarizes some essential radio terminology and their meanings:

TERM	MEANING	EXPLANATION
Analog	Continuous representation of information.	Data representation as a continuous signal, typical of traditional radio waves.
Antenna	Converts electrical signals into radio waves for transmission and vice versa for reception.	A device that sends or receives radio signals wirelessly.
APRS (Automatic Packet Reporting System)	Digital system for real-time data transmission, GPS tracking, and messaging over amateur radio frequencies.	A network for transmitting data, tracking locations, and messaging using amateur radio frequencies.

TERM	MEANING	EXPLANATION
Bandwidth	The range of frequencies within a given band is typically measured in Hertz (Hz) or kilohertz (kHz).	The spectrum of frequencies available for signal transmission within a specific range.
Beacon	The transmitter emits periodic signals for navigation, identification, or monitoring.	A device that sends signals at regular intervals for specific purposes like navigation or identification.
Beacon Station	Fixed transmitter periodically transmitting signals for navigation or propagation studies.	A stationary transmitter that sends signals periodically for specific purposes such as navigation or research.
Call Sign	A unique identifier is assigned to a radio station or operator for identification.	A distinct name or code is used to identify a radio station or user.
Carrier Frequency	The specific frequency of the unmodulated signal before modulation.	The base frequency of a signal before any changes or encoding.
CTCSS (Continuous Tone-Coded Squelch System)	Filters signals based on a sub-audible tone code to reduce interference from other users on the same frequency.	A method of blocking unwanted signals by using specific tone codes.
Decryption	Process of decoding encrypted information back into its original form.	Converting coded data back into its original, readable format.
Demodulation	Extracting the original information from a modulated carrier signal.	Recovering the encoded information from a modulated radio wave for interpretation.
Digital	Discrete representation of information.	Data representation as distinct values (0s and 1s), is common in modern digital systems.
Duplex Operation	Mode where a device can transmit and receive simultaneously, commonly used in repeater systems.	Communication mode enables devices to send and receive signals at the same time, often used in repeater setups.

TERM	MEANING	EXPLANATION
Encryption	Process of encoding information to ensure secure communication.	Converting data into a coded format to prevent unauthorized access.
Escalation Procedures	Protocols for escalating communication issues or emergencies.	Guidelines for handling and elevating communication problems or urgent situations.
Frequency	The number of times a wave oscillates in one second is measured in Hertz (Hz).	How fast a radio wave vibrates per second, determines the signal's frequency.
Frequency Modulation (FM)	Modulating the frequency of the carrier signal to encode information.	Using changes in a signal's frequency to transmit data or voice.
Gain	The measure of an antenna's ability to direct or concentrate radiation is usually expressed in decibels (dB).	The antenna's capacity to focus signal strength in a particular direction.
Ground Plane	Antenna design using a conducting surface as a ground reference to improve performance and radiation pattern.	An antenna setup that uses a surface as a reference point to enhance signal quality and coverage.
Interference	Unwanted signals or noise disrupt communication, caused by other transmitters or environmental factors.	Disturbances that disrupt radio signals, often due to other electronic devices or natural phenomena.
Interference Mitigation	Techniques for reducing or eliminating signal interference.	Methods to minimize or remove disruptions in radio communication.
LOS (Line of Sight)	Straight path between a transmitter and receiver without obstruction, crucial for VHF/UHF communications.	The direct path between two radio devices without obstacles is vital for clear communication at higher frequencies.
Modulation	Varying a carrier signal's properties (such as amplitude, frequency, or phase) to transmit information.	Changing certain aspects of a radio wave to encode data or voice for transmission.

TERM	MEANING	EXPLANATION
Power Output	The strength of the transmitted signal is typically measured in watts (W) or milliwatts (mW).	The intensity of the signal being broadcast.
PTT (Push-To-Talk)	Button or switch that activates the transmitter for sending a message when pressed.	A control to start transmitting a message.
Propagation	The way radio waves travel from a transmitter to a receiver is influenced by factors like frequency and terrain.	The method by which radio waves travel and spread is affected by various environmental factors.
QSL Card	Confirmation of a radio contact exchanged between amateur radio operators.	A card verifying communication between amateur radio users.
Receiver	Captures and converts radio frequency signals from the antenna into electrical signals for processing.	Equipment that picks up and processes radio signals for interpretation.
Repeater	Receives signals on one frequency and retransmits them on another frequency to extend communication range.	A device that boosts radio signals for wider coverage.
RF	Electromagnetic interference caused by radio signals disrupts electronic devices or communication systems.	Disturbance is created by radio signals interfering with other electronics or communication systems.
Safety/Service Tone Codes	Coded signals are used for safety or service-related communications.	Specific tones are employed for safety or service messages on radio channels.
Scanner	The receiver scans multiple frequencies or channels sequentially to monitor different communications.	A device that sequentially monitors various radio frequencies or channels.

TERM	MEANING	EXPLANATION
Simplex Operation	Mode where a device can only transmit or receive at any given time, not simultaneously.	Communication mode allows devices to either send or receive signals, but not both at once.
Single Sideband (SSB)	Suppressing one sideband of the AM signal to reduce bandwidth and increase efficiency.	Removing redundant parts of an AM signal to conserve bandwidth and improve transmission efficiency.
Squelch	Circuit that suppresses background noise when no useful signal is present, improving audio quality.	A feature that reduces noise when there's no active signal.
SWL (Shortwave Listening)	The hobby of listening to shortwave radio broadcasts for entertainment or information.	Engaging in the activity of tuning in to shortwave radio stations for enjoyment or information gathering.
SWR (Standing Wave Ratio)	Measure how efficiently the antenna system matches the transmitter's output impedance.	A metric indicating how well the antenna system matches the radio's signal output.
Transceiver	Combined transmitter and receiver devices, allowing both transmitting and receiving functions.	An all-in-one device capable of sending and receiving radio signals.
Transmitter	Generates and amplifies radio frequency signals for transmission through an antenna.	Equipment that broadcasts radio signals.
VOX (Voice Operated Switch)	Feature that activates the transmitter automatically when it detects voice input, eliminating the need for PTT.	A function that starts transmission based on voice detection, without pressing PTT.

And, just to add an extra layer, here are some commonly used tech terms related to Baofeng radios:

ABBREVIATION	FULL NAME	DESCRIPTION
ABR	Display Illumination Time	Sets the duration for the LCD backlight to stay on, usually between 0-10 seconds.
AL-MOD	Alarm Mode	Specifies how alarms are triggered: through the radio speaker only, transmitting a cycling tone, or a specific code.
ANI-ID	Automatic Number ID	Allows setting an ID code for identification, programmed via software with a maximum digit limit.
AUTOLK	Auto Keypad Lock	Automatically locks the keypad after 15 seconds to prevent accidental key presses.
BCL	Busy Channel Lock	Prevents transmission when the selected channel is in use, avoiding interference.
BEEP	Keypad Beep	Enables a beep tone when pressing buttons for feedback.
CTCSS	Continuous Tone-Coded Squelch System	Adds tone codes to channels for creating private channels, reducing interference.
DCS	Digital Code Squelch	Similar to CTCSS but uses digital codes for channel privacy and reduced interference.
DEL-CH	Delete a Memory Channel	Allows deleting a programmed channel from the radio.
DTMFST	DTMF-Sidetone of Transmit code	Determines when DTMF Side Tones are heard from the speaker during transmissions.

ABBREVIATION	FULL NAME	DESCRIPTION
LED	Display Backlight Color	Sets the color of the display backlight for different functions like standby, receive, and transmit.
MDF-A	Channel A Display Mode	Sets how channel A is displayed: channel number, channel name, or programmed frequency.
MDF-B	Channel B Display Mode	Similar to MDF-A but for channel B.
MEM-CH	Store a Memory Channel	Saves a newly created or modified channel for quick access.
MR Mode	Channel Mode	Allows navigating between programmed channels for communication.
NOAA	Weather Receiver /Scan	Enables tuning into NOAA weather broadcasts for weather reports.
OFFSET	Frequency Offset	Sets the frequency difference between transmit and receive for repeater use.
PONMSG	Power On Message	Configures the behavior and displays a message when the radio is powered on.
PTT-ID	When to send the PTT-ID	Controls the sending of ID codes at the beginning or end of transmissions.
PTT-LT	Signal Code Sending Delay	Sets the delay in sending signal codes after pressing the PTT button.
RESET	Restore Defaults	Resets the radio to factory default settings.
ROGER	Roger Beep	Sends an end-of-transmission tone after transmissions.

ABBREVIATION	FULL NAME	DESCRIPTION
RP-STE	Squelch Tail Elimination	Reduces squelch tail noise when communicating directly between radios.
RPT-RL	Delay the squelch tail of the repeater	Delays the squelch tail when using a repeater for better communication.
SAVE	Battery Save	Saves battery by adjusting sleep cycles and wake-up cycles.
S-CODE	Signal Code	Selects a DTMF code for signaling purposes during transmissions.
SC-REV	Scanner Resume Method	Sets how scanning resumes after detecting signals: time-based, carrier-based, or search-based.
SFT-D	Frequency Shift	Enables access to repeaters by shifting transmit frequencies.
SQL	Squelch Level	Sets the sensitivity level for receiving signals and filtering out noise.
STE	Squelch Tail Elimination	Eliminates squelch tail noise during direct communications.
STEP	Frequency Step	Adjusts the frequency change when navigating frequencies.
TDR	Dual Watch, Dual Reception	Receives signals from two channels simultaneously.
TDR-AB	Transmit Selection while in Dual Watch Mode	Determines the display priority when receiving signals in Dual Watch mode.
TOT	Time-Out-Timer	Limits transmission time to prevent overuse of the radio.
TXP	Transmit Power	Sets the transmitter power level for communication.

ABBREVIATION	FULL NAME	DESCRIPTION
VFO Mode	Frequency Mode	Allows manual tuning of frequencies and direct frequency input.
VOX	Voice Level	Activates hands-free communication based on microphone sensitivity levels.
VOICE	Voice prompts function	Provides voice prompts for operational feedback.

You have to establish that unbreakable conceptual framework before you stack more skills on top. For now, focus on getting this vocabulary ingrained in your mind.

Understanding Frequencies, Channels, and Modulation

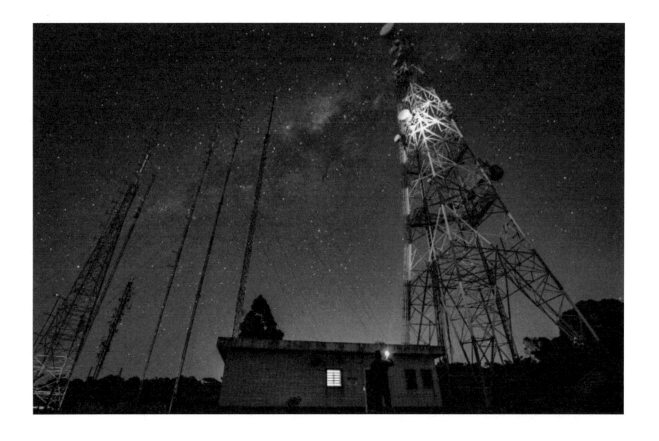

Some folks might be satisfied coasting at that 101 level of basic vocab repetition drills. Hardened operators bring that expanded insight into the field when the real lid pops off, though.

I'm talking about understanding how those frequency bands, channel protocols, and modulation schemes shape your entire radio communications world. A shallow grasp can quickly lead to critical mistakes.

Let's dissect some advanced operational specifics:

- **Frequency Bands**
  - Not all those Hertz measurements are created equal in real-world behaviors and regulatory guidelines.
  - We keep channelized frequencies organized into specific bands like VHF, UHF, LF, and the like to maintain the separation of powers across the radio waves.
  - Very High Frequency (VHF) bands typically range from 30 MHz to 300 MHz, offering better propagation through obstacles like buildings and vegetation because of longer wavelengths. VHF bands are commonly used for FM radio broadcasting, aircraft communication, maritime communication, and amateur radio.
  - Ultra-High Frequency (UHF) bands span from 300 MHz to 3 GHz, providing shorter wavelengths that enable more focused and directional signals but with reduced penetration through obstacles. UHF bands are used for television broadcasting, satellite communication, cell phones, walkie-talkies, and data transmissions.
  - Low Frequency (LF) bands generally range from 30 kHz to 300 kHz, making them longer in wavelength compared to VHF and UHF bands. LF signals have excellent ground-wave propagation capabilities, allowing them to travel long distances along the Earth's surface. This makes LF bands suitable for applications like navigation beacons, submarine communication, and long-range wireless communication in rural areas. However, LF signals are limited in bandwidth and data-carrying capacity compared to higher frequency bands like VHF and UHF.
  - By mastering these bands, you can choose the best frequency range for your specific needs and operational goals.

- **Channel Assignments**
  - Preventing total radio wave chaos requires designated channel assignment protocols.
  - Any band, whether GMRS or UHF public safety, has sliced channels specifying uplink/downlink, licensed commercial, amateur/hobbyist, and more.
  - Simplex channels handle basic unit-to-unit comms. More advanced duplex repeater pairs relay those signals across wider networks in a synchronized dance.
  - Some examples include:

- **Simplex Channels:**
  - Emergency Response: Channel 16 on marine VHF radios is designated for distress calls and emergencies at sea.
  - GMRS (General Mobile Radio Service): Channel 7 is commonly used for local family communications over short distances.
  - FRS (Family Radio Service): Channel 8 is often used for general outdoor activities like hiking or camping.
  - Programming a simplex channel:

    » Press and hold the power button until the device powers up.

    » Press the "VFO/MR" button to enter frequency mode.

    » Select the desired frequency: Use the keypad to enter the simplex frequency you want to program. For example, if the simplex frequency is 146.520 MHz, enter "146520" using the numeric keypad.

    » Press the "MENU" button, then use the arrow keys to navigate to the "TXP" (transmit power) option. Select the desired transmit power level (e.g., "H" for high power or "L" for low power) based on your communication needs.

    » Press the "MENU" button again to exit the menu, then press the "EXIT" button to return to frequency mode.

    » If you want to use a CTCSS or DCS code for privacy or interference reduction, navigate to the "T-CTCS" or "T-DCS" option in the menu and enter the desired code.

    » Press and hold the "MENU" button to enter the channel save mode. Use the arrow keys to select an empty channel slot (e.g., "01" for the first channel), then press the "MENU" button again to save the programmed settings.

    » Tune your Baofeng radio to the programmed simplex channel and test communication with another radio set to the same frequency. Ensure that both radios are using the same CTCSS/DCS code, if applicable.

- **Duplex Channels:**
  - Public Safety: Police departments may use duplex channels like 460.200 MHz (receive) and 465.200 MHz (transmit) for their communications.
  - Amateur Radio: In the 2-meter band, 146.520 MHz is a national simplex calling frequency, while duplex repeaters may operate on 146.880 MHz (-0.600 offset).

○ Commercial Radio: Business radios may use duplex channels like 462.700 MHz (receive) and 467.700 MHz (transmit) for private communications.

○ Programming a duplex channel:

» Access Programming Mode: Turn on your Baofeng radio and enter programming mode by pressing the MENU button.

» Select Frequency: Use the ▲ ▼ buttons to navigate to the frequency you want to program for the duplex channel. Make sure you have the correct frequency and offset information for the channel you are programming.

» Set Transmit Offset: Once you've selected the frequency, press the MENU button again to enter the settings for transmit offset. Use the ▲ ▼ buttons to choose the offset direction (either positive or negative) and set the offset value (typically in kHz). Confirm your selection by pressing MENU.

» Save Settings: After setting the transmit offset, press the EXIT button to save your settings and exit the programming menu.

» Set CTCSS or DCS (Optional): If your duplex channel requires CTCSS or DCS tones, you can set them by navigating to the CTCSS or DCS menu in programming mode. Use the ▲ ▼ buttons to select the desired tone and confirm your selection by pressing MENU.

» Save Channel: Once you've configured all necessary settings, press the EXIT button to save the channel programming. Your Baofeng radio is now programmed for the duplex channel with the specified frequency, offset, and optional CTCSS or DCS tones.

■ **Repeater Channels:**

○ Public Safety Extension: Repeater channels such as 462.025 MHz (receive) and 467.025 MHz (transmit) are crucial extensions for public safety agencies, enhancing coverage in urban areas and challenging terrains.

○ Amateur Radio Networks: Repeater pairs like 147.180 MHz (+0.600 offset) (receive) and 147.780 MHz (-0.600 offset) (transmit) facilitate broader amateur radio networks, enabling long-distance communications and community interactions.

○ Commercial Network Expansion: Businesses utilize repeater channels such as 462.550 MHz (receive) and 467.550 MHz (transmit) to expand their network coverage, ensuring seamless communication across large facilities or dispersed teams.

○ Programming a simplex channel:

» Press and hold the power button until the device powers up.

» Press the "VFO/MR" button to enter frequency mode.

» Use the keypad to enter the repeater frequency you want to program. For example, if the repeater frequency is 146.520 MHz, enter "146520" using the numeric keypad.

» Press the "MENU" button, then use the arrow keys to navigate to the "OFF-SET" option. Select the appropriate offset direction (positive or negative) based on the repeater's specifications. For example, if the repeater has a negative offset, choose "-".

» Navigate to the "OFFSET FREQ" option in the menu and enter the offset frequency. This value is typically provided by the repeater owner or operator. For example, if the offset frequency is 600 kHz, enter "60000" using the keypad.

» Press the "MENU" button again to exit the menu, then press the "EXIT" button to return to frequency mode.

» Program the CTCSS/DCS code: If the repeater requires a CTCSS or DCS code, navigate to the "T-CTCS" or "T-DCS" option in the menu and enter the appropriate code provided by the repeater owner.

» Press and hold the "MENU" button to enter the channel save mode. Use the arrow keys to select an empty channel slot (e.g., "01" for the first channel), then press the "MENU" button again to save the programmed settings.

» Tune your Baofeng radio to the programmed repeater channel and listen for activity. You can also key up your radio to transmit and check if your signal is being repeated by the repeater.

o Repeater channels and duplex channels are related concepts, but are not exactly the same thing:

■ **Repeater Channels:**
  o They act as relay stations, receiving signals on one frequency and retransmitting them on another frequency to extend the communication range.

  o Repeater channels are used to overcome obstacles like buildings, hills, or other terrain that would otherwise block direct communication.

  o They are essential for covering larger areas and maintaining reliable communication over distances where direct line-of-sight is not possible.

  o Repeater channels are used in public safety, amateur radio, commercial radio, and other communication systems requiring extended coverage.

- **Duplex Channels:**
  - Duplex channels allow for two-way communication, where users can both transmit and receive messages on the same channel.
  - However, duplex channels do not enable simultaneous talking and listening on the same frequency; they separate these actions to avoid interference.
  - Duplex channels are used in professional settings, public safety operations, amateur radio, and other scenarios where bidirectional communication is needed.
  - They are distinct from simplex channels, where communication occurs on the same frequency without the ability to transmit and receive simultaneously.
- Understanding these assignments keeps you compliant while leveraging optimal airways for whether you're seeking discreet conversations or connecting to the larger communication grid.

- **Modulation Techniques**
  - An invisible yet critical decision point: the modulation technique you use determines how signals are encoded and decoded for optimal performance.
  - Classic analog AM/FM modes trade robustness for simplicity. More advanced digital schemes pack extra resilience against noise/interference at higher complexity.

    - **Amplitude Modulation (AM):**
      - Modulation technique, where the amplitude of the carrier signal is varied to encode information.
      - AM varies the amplitude of the carrier wave, making it susceptible to noise and interference but suitable for long-distance transmission.
      - AM is commonly used in broadcast radio transmissions, especially for long-range communication on medium-wave and short-wave bands.

    - **Frequency Modulation (FM):**
      - Modulation technique where the frequency of the carrier signal is varied to encode information.
      - FM varies the frequency of the carrier wave, providing better resistance to noise and interference, but requiring more bandwidth.
      - FM is widely used in high-fidelity audio transmissions, FM radio broadcasting, and VHF communications due to its clarity and resistance to amplitude-based distortions.

- ○ Frequency modulation is the survivalist prepper's best friend. Optimized narrow and wideband variants ensure quality audio over the range with lower susceptibility to fading.

- ○ But we'd be naïve not to respect the unique advantages of alternative protocols for special applications like packet data bursting (a technique where data packets are transmitted in short bursts at higher speeds) or combating multipath distortion (strategies to reduce or eliminate signal degradation caused by multipath interference, where radio signals reach the receiver via multiple paths, causing phase shifts and signal cancellations).

Merely knowing the terminology without understanding the underlying concepts is a sure way to get overwhelmed when you start using your radio in the field. Half-knowledge leads to half-assed performance when you need flawless communication during a crisis. Eradicate any gaps in your knowledge, ensuring you understand not just the terms but how they interconnect. This enables you to make precise decisions, quickly switch to clear channels, and change modulation modes on the fly to overcome heavy interference. The real currency of domain mastery.

Basic Communication Protocols and Etiquette

Frequencies, channels, modulation techniques: get the intellectual framework branded into your cortex.

Even with an encyclopedia's worth of technical terminology committed to memory, it'll all be worthless alphabet soup if you can't uphold basic procedures and on-air etiquette. Radio waves are an inherently shared medium, a finite resource where complete self-regulation and universal compliance to standardized protocols form the backbone of orderly operations.

Straying from the rules and best practices could lead to serious consequences, causing disruptions and drawing unwanted attention.

We don't make amateur mistakes here. That's why we're hammering on the basics of clear transmission discipline and situational awareness before moving forward:

- **Clear Communication**
  - This foundation stone should be self-explanatory, but you'd be amazed at how often it gets undervalued. Clear and concise language is the law.
  - You articulate every transmission with purpose, precise word selection, and a confident cadence, leaving no room for ambiguity.
  - Sloppy open-ended comms just create confusion and wasted airtime. Disciplined professionals make their point with a ruthless economy and authority. Then promptly keep quiet.
  - Tips:
    - Use clear and concise language.
    - Be purposeful, with precise wording and a confident delivery
    - Be direct and to the point
    - Allow others to respond
    - Listen actively before responding
    - Use standardized phrases and terminology
    - Avoid interruptions or overlapping transmissions
    - Use assigned callsigns and identifiers for situational awareness
    - Adhere to initiation and termination protocols
- **Proper Procedures**
  - There's a sacred choreography and sequence of operations to uphold when working on any radio channel. Deviating from SOP is unacceptable.
  - We monitor before transmitting to avoid unintended "doubling" disruptions. We use standardized procedural phrases and operational vernacular for uniformity.
  - You leverage those assigned call signs and identifiers at all times. No more of these "hey, it's me" calls that reduce situational awareness.
  - Finally, we follow established initiation and termination protocols for every single communication cycle. No exceptions and no deviations. We embrace processes.
  - It will sound something like this:
    - Operator 1: "This is Whiskey Delta Four, monitoring the channel. Over."
    - Operator 2: "Roger that, Whiskey Delta Four. This is Echo Tango Seven, checking in. Over."
    - Operator 1: "Copy, Echo Tango Seven. How's the signal strength on your end? Over."

- Operator 2: "Signal is strong, Whiskey Delta Four. Proceeding with the update. Over."

- Operator 1: "Received. Go ahead with the update, Echo Tango Seven. Over."

- Operator 2: "Updating current weather conditions: clear skies, wind speed at 10 knots. Over."

- Operator 1: "Copy that, Echo Tango Seven. Weather conditions noted. Out."

- Operator 2: "Whiskey Delta Four, Echo Tango Seven, clear and returning to monitoring. Out."

- **Radio terminology:** The phonetic alphabet and basic lingo used for radio communication:

  - **A:** Alpha
  - **B:** Bravo
  - **C:** Charlie
  - **D:** Delta
  - **E:** Echo
  - **F:** Foxtrot
  - **G:** Golf
  - **H:** Hotel
  - **I:** India
  - **J:** Juliett
  - **K:** Kilo
  - **L:** Lima
  - **M:** Mike
  - **N:** November
  - **O:** Oscar
  - **P:** Papa
  - **Q:** Quebec
  - **R:** Romeo
  - **S:** Sierra
  - **T:** Tango
  - **U:** Uniform
  - **V:** Victor
  - **W:** Whiskey
  - **X:** X-ray
  - **Y:** Yankee
  - **Z:** Zulu

TERM	MEANING
Radio Check	Requesting signal strength and clarity check.
Go Ahead	Indicates readiness to receive transmission.
Stand-by	Acknowledges the other party but delays immediate response.
Roger or Ten Four	Confirms message received and understood.
Negative	Denotes a negative response or "No."
Affirmative	Confirms a positive response or "Yes." Avoid slang like "yup" or "nope."
Say Again	Requests the re-transmission of a message.
Over	Indicates the completion of one's message, awaiting a response.
Out	Signifies the end of the conversation and clears the channel for others.
Break, Break, Break	Indicates an emergency interruption in ongoing communication.
Read you loud & clear	Confirms good signal strength and clarity.
Come in	Invites the other party to acknowledge receipt of the message.
Copy	Indicates understanding of the message.
Wilco	Means "I will comply" or acknowledge receipt and agreement.
Repeat	Indicates the need to repeat something, often followed by the message or instructions to repeat.

Respecting Channel Usage

- Every frequency and channel ecosystem exists for a reason, with regulatory guidelines and pecking orders allocating air rights for safety purposes.

- Certain channels get absolute priority for emergency service use; others for localized licensed operations and for general regional traffic.

- Your job is understanding and respecting those designations and listening before transmitting. Avoid extraneous chatter, remain apprised of priority traffic, and uphold the integrity of the system.

By now, you should be getting the overarching point. The technical aspects of radio operations only represent one facet of the game. A network is only as strong as its weakest link adhering to standards, so consider these modules your informal induction into the sacred brotherhood of disciplined on-air radio conduct. Breaking the rules is a line that should never be crossed, no matter what.

Focus on the mission, not personal attention. Respect procedures that keep things smooth across all channels. That's how things work at this level. Sacrifice some freedom for overall order that benefits everyone. Anything else leads to chaos.

Over and out.

Chapter 4
Becoming a Master at Baofeng Programming

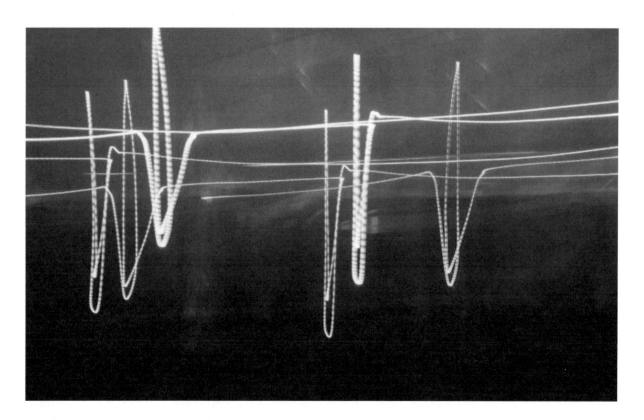

We've spent more than enough time fumbling in the shallow end, burning through the ham radio curriculum and vocabulary in basic training. That was just the warm-up to forge your mental preparedness.

This next module represents the fiery crucible separating hardened veterans in survival communications from beginners who rely on basic tools and simple call signs. A rite of passage, if you will, getting into the exclusive group of radio communication pros. And make no mistake, mastering software processes to customize your Baofeng gear isn't just about showing off your skills with the keypad. It's a foundation of knowledge that'll be incredibly valuable when you're dealing with lots of interference and noise, while others struggle to stay clear and focused.

Customized programming empowers you to bend those radio channels and modulation techniques to perfectly accommodate your specific mission parameters. Channel plans optimized for maximum coverage. Broadcasting and cross-band repeater architectures leveraging frequency combinations for range extension. Power output and bandwidth profiles are calibrated down to the decimal place. This is how big brains design comprehensive communication systems that cover everything from situation reports to coordinating field agents remotely across a whole theater of operations.

But I'm getting ahead of myself here. Let's get locked into programming.

In-Depth Guide to Programming Your Baofeng Radio for Optimal Performance

Time to embrace the barbed wire realities of true Baofeng programming mastery. Forget any delusions of grandeur. We're going in raw, understanding the intricacies of Baofeng's programming until tweaking its capabilities becomes second nature.

Channels and frequency plans don't appear magically. You need to explore those sub-menu paths to set everything just right.

The Setup Wormhole

We're mining for the advanced options here. On most Baofengs, that's via the MENU or FUNC buttons.

My advice? Get ready to dive deep into menu layers and settings for optimal custom configurations.

1. Turn on your Baofeng radio by pressing the power button. To access the menu, press the MENU button. You'll see a display with various options.

2. Use the arrow keys to navigate through the menu options. Look for settings related to frequency programming. For example, in some models, you might find this under "VFO Mode" or "Frequency Mode."

3. Let's program a common frequency used by ham radio operators for local communication: 146.520 MHz. To do this, navigate to the frequency input screen and use the numeric keypad to enter "146520" or "146.520."

4. After entering the frequency, you'll typically find an option to save or confirm your input. Select this option to save the programmed frequency.

5. Assign the programmed frequency to a channel for easy access. Navigate to the channel programming section. For example, you might see options like "Memory Channel" or "Channel Mode." Assign the frequency you programmed (146.520 MHz) to Channel 1.

6. Adjust the squelch level to filter out background noise. Look for the squelch settings in the menu. The squelch level helps to maintain clear communication by filtering out unwanted noise. Start with a moderate squelch level and adjust it based on your environment.

7. Tune your radio to Channel 1 (where you programmed 146.520 MHz). Listen for clear audio. If you hear excessive static or interference, adjust the squelch level until the audio is clear.

8. To prevent accidental changes to your settings, consider locking your programming. Look for the lock function in the menu and activate it. This ensures that your programmed frequency and channel settings remain unchanged.

Stay frosty and don't get distracted by the preferences you'll inevitably stumble across. You're after the raw channel/freq entries and transmission profiles.

Manual Frequency Entry

For all their bundled channel bank convenience, preprogrammed freqs are the McDonald's of the radio world: cheap, bloated, and ultimately unfulfilling for serious users.

That means tuning in desired frequencies via manual VFO entry down to the kHz decimal place for both VHF and UHF ranges. Take your time. Rushing these digit sequences leads to unforced errors. You'll also need to configure PL tones, power levels, and wide/narrow bandwidths accordingly. Here's an example:

1. First, turn on your Baofeng radio by pressing the power button. Once it's powered up, you'll see a screen with various numbers and icons. To access the menu, press the MENU button. This button is usually located near the top or side of the radio and may be labeled "MENU" or have an icon that looks like three horizontal lines.

2. Use the arrow keys on your Baofeng radio to navigate through the menu options. Look for an option that says something like "Frequency Mode," "VFO Mode," or "Man-

ual Input." This is the mode where you can manually enter frequencies for desired channels.

3. Depending on the type of communication you want (short-range or long-range), choose between VHF (Very High Frequency) or UHF (Ultra High Frequency) bands. VHF frequencies are typically used for short-distance communication, like within a city, while UHF frequencies are used for longer distances or in areas with obstacles, like buildings.

4. Let's say you want to program a VHF frequency of 146.520 MHz, which is commonly used by ham radio operators for local communication. Use the numeric keypad on your Baofeng radio to enter the frequency digits. For 146.520 MHz, you would enter "146520" or "146.520" depending on your radio's format.

5. After entering the frequency, look for an option to save or confirm your input. This might be labeled "Save," "Confirm," or "Enter." Press the corresponding button to save the programmed frequency to your radio's memory.

6. To test if the frequency is programmed correctly, tune your Baofeng radio to the frequency you just entered (146.520 MHz in this example). Use the arrow keys or the tuning knob to adjust the frequency until you reach 146.520 MHz. Listen for any signals or transmissions on this frequency.

7. If you want to save this frequency to a specific channel for easy access, you can do so. Navigate to the channel programming section in the menu and select an available channel (like Channel 1). Assign the programmed frequency (146.520 MHz) to this channel.

8. To prevent accidental changes to your programmed frequency, consider locking your settings. Look for a lock function in the menu and activate it. This ensures that your programmed frequency stays intact even if you accidentally press buttons.

Once satisfied, you can save these unicorns to custom channel slots for easy hot-swapping during ops.

Memory Channel Configuration

Remembering endless numeric freq sequences from scratch is a tricky endeavor. Even the gurus use rapid channel memory recollection.

But don't just accept those stock "channel 1, channel 2" preset assignments. Organize everything systematically. Banks are remapped with unique IDs based on locations and uses. Repeaters have their own allocations apart from simplex units. Modulation schemes are grouped with regulatory guidelines in mind. It's not magic, it's disciplined forethought. Make it a habit to update these memories regularly, like maintenance, instead of treating them as something unchangeable.

1. Start by turning on your Baofeng radio using the power button. Once it's on, press the MENU button to enter the menu mode.

2. Use the arrow keys on your Baofeng radio to navigate through the menu options. Look for an option that says "Channel Mode," "Memory Mode," or "Memory Channels." This mode allows you to save programmed frequencies into memory slots for quick access.

3. In the channel mode menu, you'll see a list of memory slots labeled Channel 1, Channel 2, and so on. Select an empty memory slot where you want to save your programmed frequency. For example, choose Channel 1 if it's empty.

4. Once you've selected an empty memory slot, you'll be prompted to assign a frequency to it. Use the numeric keypad on your Baofeng radio to enter the frequency digits. For example, if you want to save the frequency 146.520 MHz, enter "146520" or "146.520" depending on your radio's format.

5. After entering the frequency, look for an option to save or confirm your input. This might be labeled "Save," "Confirm," or "Enter." Press the corresponding button to save the programmed frequency to the selected memory slot (like Channel 1).

6. To test if the channel is saved correctly, exit the menu mode and tune your Baofeng radio to the saved channel (like Channel 1). Use the arrow keys or the tuning knob to select the saved channel. You should hear the programmed frequency when tuned to this channel.

7. If you want to give a custom name or label to the saved channel for easier identification, some Baofeng radios allow you to rename channels. Navigate to the channel settings menu and look for an option like "Rename Channel" or "Label Channel."

8. To prevent accidental changes to your saved channels, consider locking your settings. Look for a lock function in the menu and activate it. This ensures that your programmed channels stay intact even if you accidentally press buttons.

Repeater Offset Finessing

Unless you're locked into basic unit-to-unit traffic with limited range, live and breathe by leveraging that repeater infrastructure. But it requires some massaging; calculating and programming the specified positive and negative offsets for each repeater pair to minimize degradation.

1. Begin by turning on your Baofeng radio using the power button. Once powered up, press the MENU button to access the menu.

2. Using the arrow keys or navigation buttons, scroll through the menu options until you find the settings related to repeater operations. Look for terms like "Repeater Settings," "Repeater Offset," or "Duplex Mode."

3. Before proceeding, it's essential to understand repeater offsets. Repeaters receive signals on one frequency and simultaneously retransmit them on a different frequency to extend the range of communication. This offset frequency varies depending on the band and region but is commonly known as the repeater offset.

4. Baofeng radios typically support dual-band operation (VHF/UHF). Choose the band (VHF or UHF) you intend to use with repeaters. Then, select the offset direction based on your region's standard. Common offset directions are "+ Offset" for transmitting frequencies higher than the receive frequency and "- Offset" for transmitting frequencies lower than the receive frequency.

5. Once you've selected the band and offset direction, enter the specific offset frequency. This frequency is often present in radios for common repeater usage. However, if you need to manually enter the offset, use the numeric keypad to input the offset value in megahertz (MHz). For example, a common VHF offset is 0.600 MHz, and a UHF offset is 5.000 MHz.

6. After entering the repeater offset, save your settings by selecting the "Save," "Confirm," or "Enter" option in the menu. This ensures that your Baofeng radio remembers the configured repeater offset for future use.

7. To verify that the repeater offset is correctly set, tune your Baofeng radio to a repeater's input frequency. Transmit a test signal and listen for the repeater's response. If communication is successful, you've configured the repeater offset correctly.

8. If communication through the repeater is unsuccessful, double-check the offset direction and frequency. Make adjustments as needed until reliable communication through repeaters is achieved.

Get sloppy on these offset configs, and your range-punching capabilities become limited at best, intermittent, and garbled from multipath distortion at worst. The goal is to perfect these offset dances until repeater hopping becomes second nature.

For now, focus on internalizing these process fundamentals: menu wormholing, manual channel punching, intelligent memory mapping, and repeater offset synchronization. These are the foundational skills that summon radio prowess from the depths of technology. While some may call it mere "programming," we know it's a blend of art and science, respecting the journey of customization that leads to communication excellence.

So lock it in, byte by precious byte.

Programming Channels and Frequencies Manually

Real comms mastery demands getting elbow-deep in the raw transmission; channels and frequencies configured down to the decimal place. It's like upgrading from stock grocery store cuts to premium-aged modulation wagyu of the radio world.

It's time to embrace the art of manual channel programming. No more reliance on manufacturer generalities or uncle-approved "channel plans" cooked up for the mainstream masses.

This is how you turn those Baofeng rigs into a seamless extension of your own sharp, well-trained mind.

Frequency Band Selection

The first critical decision gate: picking your theater of operations within those neatly segmented spectral regimes such as VHF, UHF, LMR, and the like.

Each zone has its own unique coverage behaviors, regulatory considerations, and permitted allocations. Straying outside your authorized zone can lead to serious consequences.

So start by getting familiar with local channel assignment bylaws and lawful modulation limits specific to your area. Maximum power outputs, license prerequisites, all that boring stuff that separates scripts from professionals.

Let's summarize:

- **Understand Spectrum Zones**
  - Learn about VHF (Very High Frequency) and UHF (Ultra High Frequency) bands, as these are commonly used by ham radio operators.
  - Explore LMR (Land Mobile Radio) frequencies if you plan to communicate within a specific local or regional network.

- **Research Local Regulations**
  - Familiarize yourself with local laws and regulations governing amateur radio operations.
  - Look for information on authorized frequency bands, maximum power outputs, and permissible modulation types.

- **Identify Communication Needs**
  - Determine the range you need to cover based on your communication objectives.

- o Consider potential interference sources in your area, such as other radio users or electronic devices.

- **Consult Frequency Allocation Charts**
  - o Access frequency allocation charts provided by regulatory bodies like the FCC (Federal Communications Commission) in the United States or equivalent agencies in your country.
  - o Identify frequency bands allocated for amateur radio use within your region.

- **Select Appropriate Frequencies**
  - o Choose frequencies within authorized bands that suit your communication needs and offer minimal interference.
  - o Note channel spacing and separation requirements to avoid signal overlap or interference with adjacent channels.

- **Consider Modulation Limits**
  - o Understand lawful modulation limits for your chosen frequency bands.
  - o Ensure your Baofeng radio is set to operate within these modulation limits to comply with regulations.

- **Check License Requirements**
  - o Determine if a ham radio license is required in your country or region for the frequencies you plan to use.
  - o Obtain the necessary license if mandated by local regulations.

- **Set Power Output Levels**
  - o Adjust the power output of your Baofeng radio to comply with the maximum allowable levels specified by regulations.
  - o Higher power outputs may require additional licensing or authorization in some cases.

- **Document and Verify Settings**
  - o Keep a record of the frequencies, power levels, and modulation settings programmed into your Baofeng radio.
  - o Verify that your radio settings align with local regulations before transmitting.

- **Continuous Learning and Compliance**
  - o Stay updated with changes in frequency allocations and regulatory requirements.
  - o Regularly review and adjust your radio settings to ensure ongoing compliance with local regulations.

Channel Nomenclature Designations

Forget about cute nicknames or meaningless numeric IDs cribbed from built-in channel plans. We respect the art of systematic channel naming conventions.

Frequencies get meticulously labeled with operational context front and center; geographic identifiers, repeater associations, encryption schemes, and any other metadata required for immediate visual comprehension.

1. Familiarize yourself with the concept of channels on your Baofeng radio. Channels are pre-programmed frequencies you can save and access easily.

2. Decide on categories for your channels based on your communication needs. For example, you might have separate categories for local repeaters, emergency channels, and favorite frequencies.

3. Enter the manual programming mode on your Baofeng radio. This typically involves pressing a specific button combination, such as the "VFO/MR" button, followed by the "MENU" button.

4. Use the numeric keypad to assign numbers to your channels based on their priority or usage frequency. Start with Channel 1 for your most frequently used frequency or emergency channel.

5. While in manual programming mode, use the menu options to navigate to the channel name settings. This is usually found under the "Settings" or "Channel" menu.

6. Use the alphanumeric keypad to input a descriptive name for each channel. For example, "Local Repeater" for a repeater frequency used in your area.

7. After naming each channel, use the menu options to input the frequency associated with that channel. This ensures that the frequency is displayed alongside the channel name when you access it later.

8. If channel names are limited in characters, use abbreviations or short descriptors to convey the essential information. For instance, "Emergency" for emergency channels.

9. Use the menu options to organize your channels into categories or groups based on their functions or usage. This makes it easier to navigate through your channel list later.

10. Arrange your channels in order of priority or usage frequency within each category. This ensures that critical channels like emergency frequencies or frequently used repeaters are easily accessible.

11. Review your channel list to avoid duplicating channels or naming channels with similar functions redundantly. Keep your channel list concise and organized.

12. Once you have named, organized, and assigned frequencies to your channels, use the menu options to save and confirm your settings. This finalizes the manual programming process on your Baofeng radio.

13. Keep a written record or digital document of your channel names, frequencies, and purposes for reference and future programming.

14. Periodically review your channel organization to ensure it meets your evolving communication needs. Update channel names or frequencies as needed.

The real gurus even get granular by sub-categorizing channel groupings into intelligently segregated banks for different modulation types or usages. It's not just naming; it's creating a structured visual system.

Squelch Threshold Calibrations

Executing those squelch presets with strategic intent and codified battlefield doctrine is where pros separate from amateurs.

Adjust squelch settings based on modulation types and surrounding noise levels to maintain clear transmissions and reduce interference. This involves configuring carrier and CTScan tone-coded filters, adapting to varying conditions, and accounting for terrain influences on signal propagation. These adjustments are pre-planned and incorporated into our noise-reduction strategies for peak performance.

1. A squelch is a feature that mutes or suppresses audio output when the received signal strength falls below a certain threshold. It helps filter out background noise and interference when no valid signal is present.

2. Enter the menu mode on your Baofeng radio by pressing the MENU button or following the designated button combination.

3. Navigate to the squelch settings menu, which is often found under the "Settings," "Function," or "SQ" menu options.

4. Use the arrow keys or numeric keypad to adjust the squelch level. Lower levels (e.g., 0-1) are more sensitive and may pick up weaker signals but also more background noise. Higher levels (e.g., 5-9) reduce background noise but might mute weaker signals.

5. Tune your Baofeng radio to a frequency where you typically experience interference or background noise.

6. Adjust the squelch level gradually while monitoring the audio output. Find the threshold where background noise is minimized without affecting signal clarity.

7. Once you've found the optimal squelch level, save your settings using the menu options. This ensures that your squelch settings are kept for future use.

8. Some Baofeng radios offer different squelch modes, such as "Carrier Squelch" (CSQ) and "CTCSS/DCS Squelch." CSQ opens the squelch based on signal strength, while CTCSS/DCS Squelch requires a specific sub-audible tone or digital code for the squelch to open. Choose the mode that best suits your communication needs.

9. Periodically revisit your squelch settings to fine-tune them based on changing environmental conditions or communication requirements. Adjust the squelch level accordingly to maintain clear reception while minimizing background noise.

10. Keep a record of your preferred squelch settings, especially if you operate in different locations or scenarios where squelch adjustments may vary.

11. If you share your Baofeng radio with others or operate in a group setting, educate fellow users about squelch settings and how to adjust them for optimal communication quality.

Bandwidth, PL Tone, and Freq Offset Assignments

This intricate process of programming and fine-tuning delves deep into the technical aspects of transmission architectures.

Marrying the ideal bandwidth levels with corresponding PL tone frequencies for privacy encoding/decoding and interference suppression and factoring in repeater offset entrances/exits for duplex reception—all these supplementary parameters need to be defined, and performance-optimized values etched into the channel assignments. It's not about slapping a frequency on and praying for surgical precision.

1. **Bandwidth Settings**

    a. Understand bandwidth as the range of frequencies within which your radio transmits and receives signals.

    b. Access the menu mode on your Baofeng radio and navigate to the bandwidth settings, often found under "Settings" or "Bandwidth" options.

    c. Adjust the bandwidth settings based on your communication needs. Narrower bandwidths conserve power but may limit audio quality, while wider bandwidths offer better audio but consume more power.

2. **PL (Private Line) Tone Settings**

   a. PL tones, also known as CTCSS (Continuous Tone-Coded Squelch System) or sub-audible tones, are used to selectively filter out unwanted signals based on specific tones.

   b. Enter the menu mode on your Baofeng radio and navigate to the PL tone settings, usually found under "Settings," "CTCSS," or "Tone" options.

   c. Select the appropriate PL tone for the frequency or repeater you wish to communicate with. Ensure that both transmitting and receiving stations use the same PL tone to establish communication.

3. **Frequency Offset Assignments**

   a. Frequency offset is used in repeater operations to separate the transmit and receive frequencies, preventing interference.

   b. Access the menu mode on your Baofeng radio and navigate to the frequency offset settings, often found under "Settings," "Repeater," or "Offset" options.

   c. Choose the appropriate frequency offset direction (+ or -) based on the repeater's requirements. Common offsets for VHF and UHF bands are 0.600 MHz and 5.000 MHz, respectively.

   d. Input the frequency offset value in megahertz (MHz) using the numeric keypad. Double-check the offset direction and value to ensure proper repeater communication.

4. **Testing and Confirmation**

   a. After adjusting Bandwidth, PL Tone, and Frequency Offset settings, test your radio's functionality by transmitting and receiving signals on designated frequencies.

   b. Confirm that your radio operates within legal limits and complies with local regulations regarding bandwidth, PL tones, and frequency offsets.

5. **Documentation and Maintenance**

   a. Keep a record of your Bandwidth, PL Tone, and Frequency Offset settings for reference and future programming adjustments.

   b. Regularly review and update these settings as needed based on changing communication requirements or environmental conditions.

Radio professionals don't just blindly accept those presets and call it a day. Take the time and dive headlong into carving out a personalized frequency-scape tailored to your operating environments and needs. It might come across as micromanagement bordering on OCD, but it's the only path to true spectrum mastery.

So, embrace your inner control freak because every sloppy variable left un-tweaked and un-accounted for breeds unnecessary interference.

Lock it in.

Using Software and Cables for Programming Efficiency

Anyone worth their weight in coding knows there's a faster path for optimizing those channel plans. One that cuts through the wrist-destroying menu systems in favor of true software-defined radio power.

You can easily weaponize your computer skill set by exploiting purpose-built radio programming suites and PC interconnectivity protocols. This will prevent you from getting bogged down hunting-and-pecking frequencies one agonizing digit at a time.

Programming Software Installations

The first step is acquiring the software ammo for your specific hardware stack. Programming software refers to specialized tools designed to simplify the programming process for Baofeng radios.

These software tools offer a user-friendly interface with intuitive controls, making it easier to input frequencies, set channels, and manage radio settings. CHIRP is a solid open-source multi-rig option. It supports a wide range of Baofeng radio models and allows users to download and upload channel configurations, making programming faster and more convenient. With CHIRP, users can organize channels into banks, add custom names and frequencies, and import/export settings for backup or sharing with others.

Expect a steep learning curve with proprietary UIs (user interfaces) and workflow quirks based on different vendor ideologies. The khaki-green software struggle is real. But the payoff is accessing robust batch channel editing capabilities beyond your wildest menu system fantasies. The following ideas and factors will help you get started.

- Baofeng radios may also come with manufacturer-specific programming software designed specifically for their radio models.

- This software provides additional features tailored to Baofeng radios, such as firmware updates, advanced programming options, and compatibility with proprietary accessories.

- You can connect your Baofeng radio to a computer using a programming cable to access and modify radio settings using the manufacturer's software.

- Programming software offers a more intuitive and user-friendly interface compared to manual programming methods on the radio.

- Software tools like CHIRP allow users to quickly import and export channel configurations, saving time and effort.

- Software-based programming reduces the risk of human errors commonly encountered during manual programming.

- Some software tools provide advanced features like frequency scanning, channel grouping, and compatibility with external databases for repeater information.

- A programming cable is a crucial accessory that connects your Baofeng radio to a computer for programming purposes.

- These cables typically have a USB connector on one end for the computer and a connector compatible with your Baofeng radio on the other end.

- Using a programming cable and software, users can easily transfer channel configurations, update firmware, and customize radio settings without manual input on the radio's keypad.

- Download the appropriate programming software (like CHIRP for Baofeng's software) from the official website or reputable sources.

- Install the software on your computer following the provided instructions.

- Connect your Baofeng radio to the computer using a compatible programming cable.

- Launch the programming software and follow the on-screen instructions to read, modify, and write channel configurations to your Baofeng radio.

Scope it all out and pick your code craft.

Cabling Up for the Rig Interface

For most Baofeng radios, you'll need to acquire a specific serial or USB programming cradle. Once obtained, follow the manufacturer's instructions to install the required data and audio drivers on your computer.

This ensures seamless communication between your radio and the programming software. It's crucial to ensure that the cables you use match both your specific radio model and the software suite you're using. Compatibility issues can lead to frustrating firmware issues, so it's worth double-checking to avoid potential headaches down the line.

1. Select a programming cable or adapter compatible with your Baofeng radio model and computer's USB port. Ensure it's designed for programming purposes and not just for charging.

2. Plug one end of the programming cable into the USB port of your computer. Feel that satisfying click as it slots in, ready to interface with the digital world.

3. Locate the programming port on your Baofeng radio. It's often found on the side or back.

4. Connect the other end of the programming cable to the programming port on your Baofeng radio. Embrace that moment of connection, where digital and analog worlds converge.

5. If you're diving deep into firmware updates or advanced programming, ensure your Baofeng radio is powered off before connecting the programming cable. Safety first in this digital dance.

6. With your Baofeng radio and computer united by the programming cable, launch your chosen programming software. Whether it's the reliable CHIRP for Baofeng's proprietary software, let the digital symphony begin.

7. Follow the software's instructions to establish communication between your Baofeng radio and the computer. This often involves selecting the correct COM port and radio model, akin to tuning an instrument for a perfect pitch.

8. Once connected, you're ready to exchange data between your Baofeng radio and computer. Import frequencies, configure channels, and customize settings.

9. After programming your Baofeng radio, save your configurations and savor the satisfaction of a successful connection. Your radio is now tuned to your digital desires, ready to broadcast your signals across the airwaves.

Exporting and Radio Interfacing

But all these digital input line hassles are for naught if you can't successfully obey the final ritual: writing those configs from machine to radio.

Master the export commands first by verifying all your channel plans and removing any unnecessary clutter. Then, connect to the interface protocols for a mass channel upload. Welcome to the digital dojo:

1. Arm yourself with the programming software of your choice, like CHIRP for Baofeng's dedicated software.

2. Compile your desired frequencies and channel settings in a list. Whether it's local repeaters, emergency channels, or tactical frequencies, have them at the ready.

3. Launch your chosen programming software and connect your Baofeng radios using the programming cables.

4. Explore the software's batch-programming capabilities. Look for features like "Import Channels" or "Batch Configuration" that allow you to upload multiple settings at once.

5. Import your master list of frequencies and channel settings into the software.

a. In the programming software, import your master list of frequencies, channel settings, and other parameters. This master list serves as your blueprint for configuring the radio.

b. Connect your Baofeng radio to the computer using the programming cable. Feel the digital handshake as the two devices establish communication.

c. In the programming software, navigate to the section where you can write configurations for the radio. This is often labeled as "Upload to Radio" or a similar term.

d. Choose the specific configurations you want to transfer from your computer to the Baofeng radio. This could include frequencies, channel names, squelch settings, and more.

e. With your configurations selected, initiate the upload command in the programming software. Watch as the software transfers the settings from your computer to the Baofeng radio.

6. Review the batch-programmed settings to ensure accuracy. Double-check frequencies, channel names, and other parameters to avoid any skirmishes on the digital battlefield.

7. Once satisfied, initiate the upload command. Watch as your Baofeng radios transform, each one now armed with the synchronized frequencies and configurations from your master list.

8. Conduct a validation check across your batch-programmed radios. Test communication, scan channels, and verify settings to confirm operational readiness.

9. Document your batch-programmed configurations for future reference. Keep a digital record or printout of frequencies, channels, and settings for each radio in your arsenal.

Just persevere and you'll master the art of precisely manipulating electromagnetic waves.

If you think you're ready to run full unchecked comms in the field, you're in for a rude awakening. Securing your radio communications is just as mission-critical as mastering the mechanics. One sloppy breach exposing traffic to unwanted eyes and ears could completely compromise your operations or get you rolled up by the authorities for unlawful transmitting. Let's open this can of worms.

Chapter 5
Securing Your Communications

Having a loud and obvious comm signal is like painting a target on you and your crew.

That's why this entire chapter is devoted to running a full-scope security audit on your Baofeng radio comms game. We're locking it down tight to ensure zero strays that could enable hostile exploitation or monitoring. No surveillance van bagging your frequency fingerprints. No alphabet soups capitalizing on your metadata exhaust. Just you and your crew operating completely off the grid in the most fundamental sense of that phrase's existence.

Lock it in and feel the signal security. Monitoring that radiowave is about to become someone else's paranoid nightmare.

The Importance of Securing Your Communication Channels

Alright, it's time to face the harsh truth about the cyber world we're working in.

This isn't some weekend hobby where you can skate by with casual disregard for security protocols. We're playing the radio waves in increasingly hostile territory; call it the forever war zone, if you will. Out there in that digital wild, every unencrypted transmission represents a potential bleeding Achilles vector for exploitation. Whether you're hiding tactical operations or just trying to avoid attention for unregistered ham activities, the threats are constant from all angles.

Threat Vectors Inbound

Let's start by addressing your paranoia about those three-letter agencies and their relentless signal intelligence surveillance. They're not the only ones you need to worry about.

Enemy nation-state operatives are constantly on the lookout for crucial RF emissions to locate valuable targets. Criminal organizations are also a threat. Then there are the everyday nuisances: nosy neighbors, random radio hobbyists, and that opportunistic eavesdropper next door. Physical tampering and supply chain infiltrations are actual threats, too. One compromised radio in your setup can spell disaster.

- **Be aware of eavesdropping risks:** Stay vigilant for unauthorized listeners trying to intercept your communications.
  - Example: If you're discussing sensitive information like coordinates or plans over the radio, be cautious of unauthorized individuals who may be listening in. Use coded language or secure channels when necessary.

- **Guard against interception:** Encrypt sensitive transmissions to prevent unauthorized access.
  - Example: Encrypting your transmissions using digital modes like P25 (Project 25) or DMR (Digital Mobile Radio) can prevent unauthorized interception, ensuring that only intended recipients can decode and understand your messages.

- **Secure your communication channels:** Use authentication measures to ensure that only authorized users can access your channels.
  - Example: Implementing access control features such as tone squelch (CTCSS) or digital squelch codes (DCS) on your Baofeng radio can restrict access to specific channels, preventing unauthorized users from transmitting on them.

Prioritizing Information Security

Communications security, or COMSEC, is all about calculated data discretion. Every spoken syllable, every frequency twitch, is a potential giveaway of sensitive details.

Seemingly harmless details like call signs, location hints, and plans for assisted passage can give away a lot to eavesdroppers. That's why you need to guard outgoing info just as fiercely as you protect incoming transmissions. Because one breach ruins the continuity of any operation.

- **Protect personal details:**
  - Avoid sharing full names, addresses, phone numbers, or other personal identifiers over the radio to protect against identity theft or unauthorized access to personal information.
  - Use call signs or nicknames instead.

- **Secure location data:**
  - Be cautious when discussing your current location or travel plans over the radio.
  - Use general terms or codes to describe locations and avoid disclosing precise coordinates unless necessary. This prevents potential tracking or targeting by unauthorized listeners.

- **Operational security measures:**
  - Refrain from sharing detailed operational plans, schedules, or critical mission information over open radio channels.
  - Use secure channels or encrypted communication modes when discussing sensitive operational matters to maintain operational security and prevent adversaries from intercepting or disrupting plans.

- **Encryption and authentication:**
  - Consider using encryption features available in some Baofeng radios or external encryption devices to secure your communications.

  - Encryption scrambles your transmissions, making them unreadable to unauthorized listeners.

  - Use authentication measures such as tone squelch (CTCSS) or digital squelch codes (DCS) to ensure that only authorized users can access your channels.

- **Operational security best practices:**
  - Implement a "need-to-know" policy, where sensitive information is only shared with individuals who require it for operational purposes. This minimizes the risk of leaks or unauthorized disclosures.

  - Regularly review and update your communication protocols and security practices to adapt to evolving threats and technologies.

  - Stay informed about radio frequency regulations and guidelines to ensure compliance and avoid unintentional breaches of security or privacy.

Preserving Tactical Superiority

Safeguarding those transmission channels ensures you maintain radio superiority in any situation, maximizing your combat effectiveness.

Whether executing dispersed off-grid maneuvers or conventional infantry ops, uncompromised communications grant tactical advantages the adversary lacks. From issuing orders and relaying situational intel to coordinating combined arms assaults, unsecured comms inevitably deteriorate into noise and chaos once compromised. So hardline communications security remains an integral part of establishing any credible force projection capability. Lose the edge, lose the exchange.

The following tips will help you maintain and preserve tactical security:

- **Operational silence:** Keep radio transmissions concise and avoid unnecessary chatter that could reveal sensitive information or operational details.

- **Secure communication channels:** Utilize secure communication channels or frequencies to prevent unauthorized interception or eavesdropping, especially during critical operations.

- **Code words and encryption:** Use code words or encryption to convey sensitive information securely, ensuring that critical details remain confidential and are only accessible to authorized personnel.

- **Limit broadcasts:** Limit the broadcast of sensitive information, tactical plans, or operational details over open radio channels to prevent adversaries from gaining strategic advantages or compromising operational security.

- **Situational awareness:** Maintain situational awareness while communicating over the radio, being mindful of potential adversaries or eavesdroppers who may attempt to gather intelligence or exploit vulnerabilities in communication.

- **Frequency management:** Manage radio frequencies effectively to avoid interference and ensure reliable communication, especially in congested or hostile environments.

- **Periodic checks and audits:** Conduct periodic checks and audits of communication equipment, software settings, and security measures to identify and mitigate vulnerabilities or unauthorized access.

These "paranoia principles" need to become reflexive. Every time you broadcast open comms, you're one degree away from exposing your entire operational grid; no exaggerations are necessary. Let's view this as a wake-up call to change how we think about modern communication. In today's world, we're all exposed to risks due to technology.

The choice seems clear. Ignoring radiowave discipline and security will make you unbearably disruptive in the airwaves.

Implementing Encryption and Privacy Measures

We're securing communications in this chapter as tightly as possible. Encryption and privacy protocols are about to become your new best friends.

To mitigate security risks, you need to understand encryption and privacy techniques to keep your communications on the down low.

Encryption Basics

Think of encryption as sending your messages through a high-tech scrambler. Without the decryption key, any intercepted transmissions are just read as indecipherable mumbo-jumbo data. But relay that coded signal to an authorized receiver holding the key, and the message unscrambles back into plain English.

It's like an impenetrable fortified wall shielding your sensitive data from unauthorized eye-balls. Only those you grant keyhole access get to access the goods inside. Everyone else is locked out, staring at gibberish on the other side of that encryption firewall.

Baofeng radios may support various encryption types, such as DES (Data Encryption Standard), AES (Advanced Encryption Standard), or DMR (Digital Mobile Radio) encryption.

Different encryption types offer varying levels of security and complexity. Encryption involves using cryptographic keys for encoding and decoding messages, highlighting the importance of proper key management for secure communication and to deter unauthorized access. Certain encryption methods incorporate authentication measures to verify users' identities before allowing access to encrypted channels, adding an extra layer of security against unauthorized access to encrypted communications.

- **Encryption activation:**
  - Activate encryption features on your Baofeng radio according to manufacturer instructions.
  - Ensure all users understand how to use encryption effectively to maintain secure communication channels.

- **Considerations:**
  - Understand the limitations and compatibility of encryption methods with your Baofeng radio model and communication setup.
  - Regularly update cryptographic keys and review encryption protocols to enhance security and adapt to evolving threats.

Secure Communication Protocols

Your Baofeng radio has hard-wired digital encryption modes like Secure Voice and legacy ciphers ready to lock down every outgoing signal with voice-masking and frequency-hopping technology.

Flip the right switches during set-up and you've activated hardcore privacy protocols, scrambling all comms with zero effort on your part.

Secure Voice (SV) is the flagship encryption tech, deploying hyper-dynamic algorithms that rapidly rotate through trillions of possible alpha-numeric permutations. They'd have better luck deciphering the Voynich manuscript than cracking that ever-shifting cipher flow without the decryption keys. This revolving crypto-gate ensures every transmission gets its own unique identity, never repeating a single encrypted message signature for enhanced anonymity. As you know, Baofeng radios also support digital encryption modes such as DES, AES, and DMR encryption, scrambling radio transmissions. Then, there's authentication and key management, secure communication protocols to verify user identities before granting access to encrypted channels. Proper key management is crucial for securely encrypting and decrypting messages, ensuring confidentiality and integrity during communication.

- **Compatibility and configuration:**
  - Ensure that your Baofeng radio model supports and is compatible with secure communication protocols and digital encryption modes.

  - Follow manufacturer instructions to configure and activate encryption features effectively, maintaining secure communication channels.

Password Protection

Now we're packing on another layer of advanced OPSEC by setting access codes as the hallway security checkpoint for all your encrypted channels. These personalized passwords function as the literal keys to the encryption kingdom; no code, no admittance under any circumstances whatsoever.

No matter how skilled a hacker is at eavesdropping, they can't intercept a transmission without the correct code.

So we're locking it down with a two-stage defense: first, an impenetrable encryption scrambler to mask your message contents, then an access code stronghold preventing unauthorized users from even receiving the coded signal to begin with. Your channels become exclusive no-fly zones, completely off-limits to anyone lacking the combined encryption key and password keycards.

- **Strong passwords:**
  - Create strong passwords that are difficult to guess or brute-force attacks.
  - Use a combination of letters, numbers, and symbols, and avoid using easily guessable information, such as birthdays or common words.

- **Regular updates:**
  - This is a no-brainer; regularly update passwords to enhance security and prevent unauthorized access.
  - Change passwords periodically and avoid sharing them with unauthorized individuals.

- **Configuration and settings:**
  - Follow manufacturer guidelines to configure password protection settings on your Baofeng radio.
  - Ensure that password protection features are activated and properly configured to maximize security.

Lock it down, lock it all down. Every bit of data sent through our channels gets encrypted so tight, it's like trying to crack a safe with a toothpick. Once it's locked down, you toss it into a digital black hole, bouncing it around your network like a game of interstellar ping-pong.

Strategies for Avoiding Interception and Monitoring

Yes, we're still focused on ensuring sensitive transmissions stay secure with top-notch counter-surveillance protocols.

The following key tactics are worth a go for staying off the radar:

- **Frequency hopping:** This technique rapidly switches your transmission between different frequencies in unpredictable patterns. It prevents eavesdroppers from locking onto your signal and circumvents attempts at jamming or interception on a single frequency. Your transmission ghosts in and out too fast for them to track. On a Baofeng radio, frequency hopping may be achieved through advanced encryption modes or specialized software features. To enable frequency hopping, ensure that your Baofeng radio supports this feature and follows manufacturer instructions for configuration.

- **Stealth communication:** Sometimes lying low and minimizing transmission is the best approach. Use lower power settings and directional antennas to reduce your radio's range and electronic signature. The less you broadcast, the harder it is to detect your communications. We're talking full-on radio silence unless absolutely vital. Baofeng radios can facilitate stealth communication through encryption modes, secure channels, and low-power transmission settings. To engage in stealth communication on a Baofeng radio, activate encryption features, use secure communication channels, and adjust transmission power to minimize detection.

- **Monitoring and detection:** You need early warning systems scanning for any suspicious radio traffic that could indicate monitoring or interception attempts. Software-defined radios can sweep the spectrum for anomalies like fake noise, unexplained interference, or other signs of uninvited company on your channel. Constant vigilance is key to catching skulkers before they catch you. Baofeng radios typically feature scanning modes, signal strength indicators, and frequency monitoring options. To monitor and detect radioactivity, use the scanning function on your Baofeng radio to search for active frequencies and identify potential threats or unauthorized transmissions.

The second you detect something stray, that's when you initiate countermeasures. Go full frequency hopping mode or shut down all non-essential transmitting to evade hostile trackers. No more broadcasting openly. From now on, every single communication is a drill for maintaining radio discipline and OPSEC. You're shifting to a need-to-know, transmit-only-when-absolutely-necessary posture.

Learn frequency hopping, low observability, and proactive monitoring as soon as possible.

Chapter 6
Licensing and Legalities

We've covered all the tradecraft for operating completely off the radar. But none of those cloak-and-dagger skills means squat if you get held up by the long stick of the law for violating regulations.

That's why you need a refresher on licensing and legalities governing radio usage. Understand all the detailed regulatory frameworks to ensure that all communication activities are lawful and transparent. You can't afford to theoretically jeopardize operational security and bring unwanted scrutiny down on your whole team. You're required to run a tight unjammable channel fully compliant with federal, state, and local statutes on radio operation. Anyone operating outside legal parameters will face preventable consequences of monumental proportions. Study up and memorize it backwards and forwards, because pleading ignorance to the law won't save you from catching heat.

We're going full-on by the books, no exceptions.

Overview of FCC Regulations Regarding Radio Usage

The Federal Commissions Commission (FCC) is the big daddy overseeing and allocating every sliver of the radio frequency spectrum across the United States. They're the frequency governors ensuring no Hellcats trespass or stomp on each other's turf.

The FCC divvies up radio freqs into designated chunks for specific purposes: amateur radio, public safety, maritime, commercial broadcasts, you name it. Certain radio services, like ham radio operators, require a license from the FCC to operate legally. These licenses may have different classes or levels, each with its own privileges and responsibilities.

Part 97 regulations: This is the big book of FCC commandments explicitly covering amateur radio service that you need to memorize. We're talking licensing requirements, technical standards, operational provisions, the whole nine yards of legalese governing every aspect of your radio habits. Violate Part 97 and its penalties or license revocation. The FCC enforces regulations through monitoring, inspections, and responding to complaints of interference or non-compliance.

Equipment certification: No radio, Baofeng or otherwise, is legal for operation unless it meets strict FCC certification requirements, proving it won't blast out interference or try invading other frequency allocations. The FCC sets limits on the transmit power and antenna height for various radio services to prevent harmful interference (such as using specific modulation techniques, bandwidth restrictions, and coordination procedures) and ensures spectrum efficiency. There needs to be extensive tech inspections and standards compliance to even get your gear out of the factory door.

Any comms rig that's not carrying legitimate certification stickers is contraband, plain and simple. One team, one protocol, one book of rules—the FCC's.

Steps to Obtain the Necessary Licenses for Operating Baofeng Radios Legally

If you're hoping to fire up those Baofeng rigs and start legally transmitting, you've got some mandatory licensing hoops to jump through first.

The amateur radio license is the big kid permission slip from the FCC, allowing you to throw signals around designated amateur frequency ranges. No ham ticket, no transmitting, period. The FCC splits amateur licenses into different classes with varying privileges:

- Technician Class is the baseline entry-level, granting access to limited VHF/UHF bands
- General Class upgrades you to wider spectrum permissions
- Extra Class is full baller status with nearly all amateur frequencies unlocked

The Technician Class test is targeted at beginning hobbyists, covering must-know essentials. The General Class exam ramps up the difficulty with more advanced concepts. And the dreaded Extra Class exam? Let's just say that Monster Burger separates the dedicated diehards from the tire-kickers real quick. To earn these ascending license classes, you have to go through and pass a series of progressively harder written exams covering radio theory, rules, and regulations. No free passes.

Here are the steps to obtain the necessary licenses for operating Baofeng radios legally:

1. Begin by researching the license requirements for operating Baofeng radios in your country or region.
2. Determine the type of license needed based on your intended use, such as an amateur radio (ham) license or a commercial radio license.
3. If a licensing exam is required, study the relevant materials and prepare for the exam.
4. Familiarize yourself with radio operating procedures, regulations, and technical knowledge necessary for passing the exam.
5. Once prepared, apply for the appropriate license through the regulatory authority, such as the Federal Communications Commission (FCC) in the United States.
6. Follow the application process, which may include submitting forms, documentation, and fees.
7. If a licensing exam is required, schedule and take the exam at an approved testing location.
8. Ensure you meet the passing score criteria and obtain the necessary certification.

9. After completing the application process and any required exams, await approval from the regulatory authority.

10. Once approved, you will receive your official license, authorizing you to operate Baofeng radios legally.

11. Upon receiving your license, familiarize yourself with the regulations and guidelines outlined in your license.

12. Adhere to operating rules, frequency restrictions, power limits, and other requirements to maintain legal compliance.

These certification tests aren't impossible, but they'll probe whether you truly grasp fundamentals. Don't even think about trying to skate through these exams with half-assed preparation. The FCC proctor staff administering these tests can sniff out posers pretty damn quickly.

There's no negotiating here. Earning an amateur radio license through proper accreditation channels is the only way you're operating a Baofeng or any other transmitter legally on American soil.

Compliance with Local Laws and Regulations

On top of Big Brother FCC oversight, you've also got a tangled web of local ordinances and jurisdictional red tape restricting how, when, and where you can realistically use those radios.

- **Regional regulations:** Different states, counties, and even cities have their own added layers of rules overriding FCC guidance. We're talking about local frequency allocations, power output limitations, and noise ordinances to prevent signal interference and maintain communication quality. These limitations may vary depending on the type of radio service and the area's population density. As if we need more confusing jurisdictional songs compounding on top of federal statutes.

- **Licensing requirements:** And you thought earning an FCC amateur license was enough? Licensing requirements can be more complex than just getting an FCC amateur license. In certain areas, manufacturers may also need to apply for separate state, county, or municipal permits to legally operate radios. This means additional fees, paperwork, and potential headaches to ensure full legal compliance.

- **Interference mitigation:** Let's say you're following every FCC rule to the letter, but Nancy Numbnuts two blocks over somehow thinks your transmissions are interfering with her rabbit-ear TV. Now you've got a legal circus to resolve per local noise regulations or face violation notices and fines from the city. Some local regulations address environmental and health concerns related to radiofrequency emissions. Limits on antenna height or proximity to sensitive areas, such as schools or hospitals, may be enforced to mitigate potential risks. It's a labyrinth of overlapping, contradictory local laws, creating total regulatory hell. Situations where you could hypothetically be 100% compliant with FCC standards yet still get jammed up over some crazy town ordinance about operating radios within 500 feet of a petting zoo.

- **Coordination with authorities:** Radio operators must coordinate with local authorities and regulatory agencies to ensure compliance with all applicable laws and regulations. This may involve getting approvals, submitting documentation, and adhering to operational guidelines specified by local authorities.

The sad reality is your FCC license doesn't give you some unlimited get-out-of-jail-free card for transmitting wherever, whenever. Operating amateur radio is a meticulous chess game requiring navigating the entire legal framework from top to bottom.

Chapter 7
Advanced Operations

Field expediencies, antenna optimizations, mesh networking protocols–we're cramming it all into the cerebral hard drive.

This is the peak of the mountain where we master every last capability of these Baofeng platforms and transform into unstoppable communication juggernauts. Any amateur-hour users still struggling with rookie concepts like basic encryption better get educated ASAP. Because from here on out, we're going full in on the knowledge front.

No more playing patty-cake in the shallows. We're drowning in the deep end of advanced radio mastery, where the real operators get forged through trial by fire.

Exploring Advanced Features and Capabilities of Baofeng Radios

We're just scratching the surface by solely using basic PTT and frequency tuning. There's an entire galaxy of force-multiplying features waiting to be exploited.

- **Dual-band operation:** Top-tier Baofeng models are straight-up multi-threaded radios capable of simultaneously operating across both VHF and UHF frequencies. We're talking about completely ubiquitous spectrum coverage with no compromises at the flick of a switch. Instead of limiting yourself to one bandwidth at a time, you've got discrete channels pumping out independent transmissions on separate freq ranges concurrently. Flexibility and versatility maxed out to ludicrous levels, giving you the always-on QRP to operate seamlessly between systems and theaters. QRP refers to "Quick Reactionary Procedures" or "Quick Reaction Procedures." It suggests the ability to respond rapidly and efficiently to changing situations, particularly in terms of communication channels and frequencies.

- **Cross-band repeater functionality:** Certain innovative Baofeng variants pack powerful cross-band repeater capabilities for extending that communication footprint even further. These rigs can fully retransmit signals across frequency bands with no data loss. When coupled with dual-band mastery, you're talking about a footprint expansion where VHF traffic gets rebroadcast on UHF freqs, extending range far beyond normal limits. Same with mirroring the reverse—UHF to VHF repeating for penetrating through any terrain or environmental interference. It's like a force multiplier, launching your transmissions out to the stratosphere.

- **Emergency alert features:** These radios aren't just comms tools though; they're also designed to enhance safety and situational awareness with integrated emergency alert functionality. Every Baofeng rig taps directly into emergency services and NOAA weather/hazard networks for real-time threat notifications. If a coded alert bulletin gets broadcast over any frequency marking an impending tornado, you get that critical data packet displayed with audible and physical alarms alerting your handset. No more operating blind to clear and present environmental dangers in the area. Same with individual SOS functions, hitting responders with your exact GPS coordinates if you actually need emergency assistance.

The following table neatly outlines the advanced features and capabilities of Baofeng radios:

FEATURE	DESCRIPTION
Frequency Range	Baofeng radios typically cover a wide frequency range, including VHF (136-174 MHz) and UHF (400-520 MHz) bands.
Power Output	Baofeng radios offer adjustable power output settings, ranging from low power (1 watts) to high power (5 watts), for varying communication ranges.
Dual-Band Operation	Many Baofeng radios support dual-band operation, allowing users to transmit and receive on both VHF and UHF frequencies simultaneously.
Channel Memory	Baofeng radios feature extensive channel memory capabilities, with the ability to store hundreds of channels for quick and easy access.
CTCSS/DCS Codes	Baofeng radios support Continuous Tone-Coded Squelch System (CTCSS) and Digital-Coded Squelch (DCS) codes for selective calling and privacy.
VOX Function	Voice-activated transmission (VOX) allows hands-free operation, activating transmission automatically when speaking into the microphone.
Dual PTT	Dual Push-to-Talk (PTT) buttons enable users to switch between two channels or frequencies without changing settings, enhancing communication flexibility.
FM Radio	Many Baofeng radios include built-in FM radio receivers, allowing users to tune in to FM broadcasts for entertainment or information.
Emergency Alerts	Some Baofeng radios feature emergency alert functions, including NOAA weather alerts and programmable emergency channels for critical communications.

FEATURE	DESCRIPTION
Scanning Modes	Baofeng radios offer various scanning modes, such as priority scanning, dual-watch scanning, and scanning multiple channels for activity.
Encryption Capabilities	Advanced models may support encryption features, such as DES and AES encryption, for secure and private communication.
GPS Capability	Certain Baofeng radios come with integrated GPS capabilities, allowing users to track their location and coordinates for navigation and emergency purposes.
Bluetooth Connectivity	High-end models may offer Bluetooth connectivity for wireless communication with compatible devices, such as headsets or external speakers.

Baofeng rigs are multi-environment digital Swiss Army knives. No more basic AM/FM operations. Its full spectrum coverage, bandwidth meshing, and hyper-aware safety protocols are embedded into every future transmission.

Long-Range Communication Techniques

We've hacked and maxed out every advanced capability those Baofeng rigs can muster. But you're still functionally limited by physics itself with transmission range.

Crank up the output wattage all you want, but those radio waves are eventually getting choked out by terrain, atmospheric conditions, or the literal curvature of the planet. To become true long-range master signalers, you need to bend the rules of the terrestrial realm itself through some unorthodox methods.

Antenna Upgrades

The first force multiplier to vastly increase that broadcast reach? Ditch the ponies that ship with your radios for some higher-caliber, higher-gain antenna appliances custom-engineered to punch signals harder and farther with tighter directionality.

I'm talking about aftermarket antennas purpose-built for DX goals; focused RF radiation pattern for slicing through any obstacle or interference instead of radiating output in wasteful omnidirectional spheres. More reach, more penetration, and more decimated obstacles in the transmission path.

- Upgrade to a higher-gain antenna to extend your radio's reach and improve signal coverage, especially in open areas or long-distance communications.

- Opt for antennas designed to minimize signal loss and interference from obstacles, such as multi-element antennas or antennas with signal amplification features.

- Ensure compatibility between your Baofeng radio model and the upgraded antenna to maximize performance and avoid compatibility issues.

- Consider a directional antenna or one with a higher gain to penetrate obstacles like buildings or foliage for clearer communication in challenging environments.

- After upgrading, conduct signal tests in various locations to fine-tune antenna positioning and settings for optimal performance in different scenarios.

- Check local regulations and licensing requirements to ensure compliance when upgrading antennas, especially for higher-gain or directional antennas that may require additional approvals.

- The following summary will get you dialed in on antenna basics:

ANTENNA MODEL	FREQUENCY RANGE	GAIN	CONNECTOR TYPE	DESCRIPTION
Baofeng UV-5R Antenna	136-174 MHz (VHF), 400-520 MHz (UHF)	2.15 dBi (VHF), 3.5 dBi (UHF)	SMA-Female	Standard antenna for Baofeng UV-5R radios, offering balanced performance for both VHF and UHF frequencies.
Nagoya NA-771 Antenna	144/430 MHz	2.15 dBi	SMA-Male	High-gain antenna designed for improved reception and transmission on VHF and UHF bands.

ANTENNA MODEL	FREQUENCY RANGE	GAIN	CONNECTOR TYPE	DESCRIPTION
Tram 1185 Dual-Band Antenna	144-148 MHz (VHF), 430-450 MHz (UHF)	2.5 dB (VHF), 4.5 dB (UHF)	SMA-Female	Dual-band antenna optimized for VHF and UHF frequencies, providing enhanced gain for better signal performance.
Diamond SRH805S Antenna	144/430 MHz	2.15 dBi	SMA-Male	Compact and lightweight antenna suitable for portable use, offering outstanding performance on VHF/UHF bands.

Elevated Antenna Deployment

Every meter of altitude your antenna feed point gets elevated is one less meter wasted, with that signal refracting off the curvature of the Earth.

Trees, towers, rooftops, you need to master all the high-up deployment techniques to keep your radiation pattern firing clean over any terrain or urban clutter trying to block our golden command voice. Who needs direct line-of-sight when your signal is soaring a hundred meters above all those visual obstructions from the jump?

- Adhere to industry standards and emissions limits for antenna installations to ensure compliance and minimize unwanted radiation.

- Elevate antennas to gain a height advantage, extending coverage range and improving line-of-sight communication in flat or obstructed terrain.

- Use directional antennas and additional equipment, like reflectors or beamforming techniques, to control signal directionality and minimize unwanted radiation.

- Ensure sturdy and stable mast structures to support elevated antennas, withstand environmental conditions, and maintain a consistent radiation pattern.

- Implement proper grounding and shielding techniques to reduce electromagnetic interference and maintain a clean radiation pattern.

- Analyze the antenna's radiation pattern when elevated to align with communication objectives and minimize signal spillage or interference.

- Experiment with different heights to find the optimal elevation that maximizes coverage while maintaining a clean radiation pattern.

- Take terrain, vegetation, nearby structures, and other environmental factors into account that may affect the radiation pattern, and adjust deployment strategies accordingly.

Radio Propagation

Then we take it to the next level by hacking the actual atmospheric conditions directly to maximize signal ducting potential. We're all for special conditions like when the air is just right (tropospheric openings) or when radio waves bounce off the sky (ionospheric skip). These conditions can send our signals much farther than normal.

Thunderstorm-charged atmospheric inversions, Aurora Borealis effects, you name it. These natural events can help bounce your signals really far, almost like shooting them from a cannon. We're even using clouds and meteors to bounce our signals around obstacles, like magic beams in the sky!

- Conduct a detailed analysis of propagation paths, considering ground wave, sky wave, and line-of-sight propagation for optimal signal transmission.

- Choose frequencies strategically based on propagation characteristics, utilizing lower frequencies for longer-range ground wave propagation and higher frequencies for shorter-range line-of-sight communication.

- Align antennas precisely for maximum signal propagation, accounting for polarization, elevation angles, and azimuth direction to minimize interference and maximize signal strength.

- Adjust antenna placement and elevation to mitigate terrain effects such as shadowing, diffraction, and reflection, optimizing signal propagation in diverse environments.

- Implement techniques like antenna height elevation, signal reflection, or relay stations to mitigate signal obstructions, ensuring reliable communication in obstructed areas.

- Continuously monitor atmospheric conditions, including temperature, humidity, and ionospheric activity, to expect and adapt to changes that may impact signal propagation.

- Employ strategies to manage multipath interference, such as antenna diversity, signal amplification, or frequency modulation, maintaining signal integrity, and reducing degradation.

- Utilize signal enhancement techniques like error correction, modulation schemes, and frequency agility to optimize signal quality and overcome propagation challenges.

- Design communication systems with redundancy, backup channels, and resilient protocols to ensure continuous connectivity and communication reliability under varying propagation conditions.

- Explore advanced techniques to exploit atmospheric conditions for enhanced signal propagation, leveraging phenomena like tropospheric openings, ionospheric skip trajectories, and atmospheric disturbances to maximize signal ducting potential and extend communication ranges. Advanced techniques include:

  o **Tropospheric ducting:** Utilizes temperature inversions in the troposphere to create ducts that guide radio waves over longer distances than usual.

  o **Enhanced tropospheric propagation:** Enhances tropospheric signal propagation using atmospheric conditions, like super-refraction or ducting effects for increased signal range.

  o **Ionospheric skip propagation:** Takes advantage of ionospheric layers to bounce radio signals for long-distance communication, especially during periods of the ionospheric skip.

  o **Cloud-bounce communications:** Utilizes cloud layers as signal reflectors to extend communication ranges, particularly effective in mountainous or obstructed terrains.

  o **Meteor scatter communications:** Uses meteor trails to reflect and scatter radio signals, enabling communication over extended distances.

  o **Aurora Borealis effects:** Exploits aurora-induced ionospheric disturbances for enhanced signal propagation, particularly in polar regions during auroral events.

  o **Sporadic E propagation:** Capitalizes on sporadic ionospheric E-layer enhancements to achieve short-term, long-distance radio communication.

  o **VHF/UHF tropo ducting**: Focuses on utilizing tropospheric ducts for VHF and UHF frequencies to achieve long-range communication in favorable weather.

- Innovate with cloud-bounce communications, meteor trail electromagnetic phenomena, and other creative methods to harness natural atmospheric phenomena as makeshift signal cannons, pushing the boundaries of signal propagation capabilities.

Push power to the theoretical limits, antenna farm to the heavens, and start hacking the troposphere like a meteorology shaman. Those are the new marching orders for any dedicated long-haul communicator.

Integrating Baofeng Radios into a Larger Communication Network

We're going to be pulling out all the stops to build these independent networks. Gone are the days of isolated radio users feeling stranded.

We're using encryption, peer authentication, and multiple routing paths to create robust systems. This gives communities the ability to communicate on their own or connect with outside help in emergencies until regular communication infrastructure is back online.

We're moving towards a fully connected network where every Baofeng radio becomes a strong node in a secure, flexible system.

- **Network topologies:** No more basic "I transmit, you receive" dynamics. We're restructuring communication flows into intelligent network architectures optimized for any scenario.
  - ○ **Point-to-multipoint star:** In this setup, your Baofeng becomes a central hub relaying signals to multiple outstations in a hub-like structure, ideal for scenarios where quick connections and broad coverage are crucial.

- **Pointer:** Set up your Baofeng as the central routing node and ensure a clear line-of-sight to maximize transmission range.

○ **Mesh grids:** These are decentralized distributed transmitters forming self-healing resilient meshes impervious to single-point failures. Each Baofeng rig becomes a node, creating redundant paths for data transmission, and ensuring communication even if one node fails.

- **Pointer:** Configure your Baofeng to relay packets across multiple paths and regularly test network resilience by simulating node failures.

Encrypted peer-to-peer meshes, urban VHF/UHF hyperlinks, and LPD freq band multi-cluster clouds embrace every hardened architecture and switching protocol under the sun to maximize comms flexibility.

- **Cross-platform interoperability:** Part of unlocking true network versatility is achieving cross-platform interoperability so your Baofeng nodes can interface seamlessly with any other radio hardware or device.

○ **Pointer:** Familiarize yourself with different signal standards and encoding schemes to ensure smooth communication across various platforms.

Embed every instruction set and every transceiver firmware into your systems. Creating maps for different signal standards, encoding methods, and translation tools so that systems can process and transmit data across any communication platform, old or new, without losing information. We're aiming for professional-grade performance, not amateur-hour setups.

We're speaking a common language (lingua franca) that bridges different encryption methods, waveforms, and the worldwide communication network (unified global voice/data pipeline) whether it's Software-Defined Radios (SDRs), APCO25, NXDN, or P25 standards.

- **Community networks:** These are community-based backup networks deployed during emergencies, such as neighborhood watch clusters or NGO (backup networks set up by community-based organizations or non-governmental organizations (NGOs) during emergencies) response teams.

○ **Pointer:** Coordinate with local groups to establish backup channels and practice using them regularly to ensure readiness during crisis events.

Neighborhood watch clusters, prepper rendezvous trunks, NGO/rural 911 reserve channels—decentralized Baofeng meshes are deployed on-site for mutual aid and collaboration during emergencies. These networks are secure from common vulnerabilities.

It's not just about mastering the basics; it's about becoming an expert in designing and setting up strong communication networks using Baofeng radios. So, step up to professional-level communication or step out. Got it?

Nothing quite like a nice surprise, right? So, here's a gift for you: a solid start for your emergency preparedness. Just scan the QR code to access the exclusive Emergency Communication Plan Template and get your comms sorted. Enjoy!

Chapter 8
Troubleshooting and Maintenance

Maintaining communication superiority means treating those Baofeng rigs with the same militant ownership mentality as your issued weapon system.

Ignoring basic preventative maintenance and troubleshooting leads to catastrophic failures at the worst possible times. They aren't Tonka toys designed to withstand being chucked across rooms. Combined arms manuals even cover transportation and storage guidelines for avoiding impact shears, distortion, and moisture ingress—the whole laundry list of preventable faults. Because one link's negligence poisons the entire unit's mobile capacity through sheer rookie disuse and mishandling.

We are the "High Church of Radio Sanctity." Either buy into these dogmatic "commandments" completely or do not pass "Go."

Common Issues with Baofeng Radios and How to Troubleshoot Them

Even with our fanatical preventative maintenance, the sad reality is radios will still falter and experience malfunctions out in the field. We're going to quickly identify and fix the most common system faults before they become major signal integrity problems.

Interference and Signal Degradation

Few things cripple a comms operation quicker than externally radiated electromagnetic noise, corrupting your wavefront coherence and blasting those broadcasts into indecipherable garble. Here's a toolkit to tackle these issues:

- **Squelch setting tweaking:** Adjust the squelch threshold up or down to filter out ambient interference without losing legitimate signals.
  - **Pointer:** Experiment with different squelch levels until you find the optimal setting that minimizes interference. Too low and you're injecting a sea of white noise static. Too high and you risk dropping legit signals.

- **Frequency relocation:** If squelch can't cull the offending interference, switch to different transmission frequencies to avoid interference patterns. Even hopping just a few kHz or MHz can relocate your broadcast outside interference patterns.
  - **Pointer:** Incrementally change frequencies or use frequency hopping techniques to find a clear channel.

- **Spectrum mapping:** For hardcore cases, initiate full isotropic software-defined RF environment mapping to fingerprint the precise sources using directional attenuation and localized band recording.
  - **Pointer:** Conduct a thorough RF environment scan to identify and mitigate interference sources.

- **Noise cancellation:** Activate digital noise suppression to extract interference and improve signal clarity. We're talking real-time adaptive filters and excision algorithms.
  - ○ **Pointer:** Enable noise reduction features on your radio to enhance audio quality in noisy environments.

Battery Drain and Power Issues

That flashing low-battery light on your set is the first warning siren that your portable power situation is teetering on the brink of total system blackout. Let's probe for causes:

- **Parasitic load analysis:** Initiate full system power audit and inspect terminals, circuits, and loads for anomalies that may deplete energy reserves prematurely.
  - ○ **Pointer:** Identify and isolate any parasitic loads or short circuits that contribute to battery drain.

- **Efficiency profiling:** Optimize radio settings for energy efficiency across all channels and functions.
  - ○ **Pointer:** Adjust power settings, duty cycles, and encryption usage to maximize battery life.

- **Battery health sampling:** Monitor battery health indicators to track discharge rates, recharge cycles, electrode sediment buildup, and catastrophic depletion cliffs—no energy storage vector unchecked.
  - o **Pointer:** Regularly check battery status and replace aging batteries to maintain optimal performance.

- **Redundant failover:** In worst-case depletion scenarios, batteries immediately get hot-swapped with fresh reserves from dedicated mobile charging/conditioning lockers.
  - o **Pointer:** Keep spare batteries charged and accessible for immediate deployment when needed.

Programming Errors

A single person pressing some oblivious channel parameters or scrambling memory map allocations can digitally sabotage an entire networked comms architecture if not caught instantly.

- **Input validation parsing:** Validate user inputs to prevent errors in frequency, mode, and parameters.
  - o **Pointer:** Implement checksum calculations and syntax validation to catch and correct input errors.

- **Mapping schema validation:** Audit channel schemas. Existing channel schemas are continuously audited against global master keys to detect any type/value deviations or slot quantity overflows. Illicit programming gets remediated automatically.
  - o **Pointer:** Regularly compare channel configurations against master keys and correct any deviations.

- **Cryptographic verification**: Under no circumstances do any custom configs propagate without passing multi-layered crypto-verification against PKI-whitelisted parameters (parameters that have been approved and authorized through cryptographic verification against a set of rules) rulesets. Servers reject all non-compliant binaries. Verify custom configurations against security protocols to prevent unauthorized programming.
  - o **Pointer:** Use multi-layered crypto-verification to ensure that only compliant configurations are accepted.

- **Forensic audit trails:** Maintain logs of programming interactions for accountability and error tracing.
  - o **Pointer:** Keep detailed records of programming activities for forensic analysis and troubleshooting.

Audio Problems

A degraded voice pipeline can cripple the entire transmission cycle even with flawless wave-front propagation. We troubleshoot audio with the same militarized granularity as any other factor:

- **Microphone diagnostics:** Check microphone settings and calibration for optimal voice transmission. Every aspect of the inbound analog/digital voice conversion path gets evaluated down to the MEMS diaphragm.
  - ○ **Pointer:** Adjust sensitivity and background noise suppression to improve microphone performance.

- **Speaker diagnostics:** Outbound acoustic staging is just as crucial—impedance measurements, harmonic distortion patterns, cone degradation analysis, and the whole signal chain from DAC bits to final acoustic summation. Evaluate speaker quality and performance to ensure clear outbound audio.
  - ○ **Pointer:** Test speaker output and adjust settings to minimize distortion and improve clarity.

- **Interference mitigation:** Use digital signal processing tools to filter out background noise and interference.
  - ○ **Pointer:** Enable noise gates, comb filters, and notch suppressors to reduce unwanted noise in audio signals.

- **Circuit analysis:** When problems persist, it's time to break out the analyzers for deeper analog/digital circuit-level signal tracing on those voice pipelines. Conduct circuit-level analysis to identify and address hardware issues affecting audio quality.
  - ○ **Pointer:** Use oscilloscopes and logical analyzers (tools for circuit analysis when troubleshooting issues in audio pathways) to troubleshoot circuit-level problems in the audio pathway.

Every one of those core troubleshooting dimensions feeds directly back into our indoctrination process. When our entire digital network comes to a standstill because of a rookie mistake, it's like hitting the emergency reset button, and you can't afford that. Demand flawless performance and zero tolerance for system failures. You need to be quick and precise in fixing any issues that threaten your communication integrity. Whether it's removing interference, analyzing power usage, checking encrypted programming, or tracing audio signals, you need to be on top of it like a space wizard cyborg.

Never compromise on system integrity.

Tips for Maintaining and Prolonging the Lifespan of Your Radio

It's simple; ignoring basic preventative maintenance leads to catastrophic failures, usually at the worst possible times. We're locking it down:

- **Regular inspection & cleaning:** Your standard PMCS drill now includes full handset environmental decontamination procedures to remove any caked gunk, corrosive residue, or airborne particulate matter trying to sabotage internal componentry. Make sure your radios aren't choked by dust and dirt buildup that can block fan vents or signal paths. Think through IPC TM-650 standards (cleaning procedures for electronics) for wiping down every part of your radio. Skipping this step is not an option; it's like ignoring the real reasons for underperformance, such as dirty connectors or battery contacts. Cleaning electronics according to IPC TM-650 standards:
  - o Use a soft, lint-free cloth to wipe down the exterior surfaces of the device, including the case, ports, and buttons.

  - o Avoid using harsh chemicals or abrasive materials that could damage the device.

  - o Pay special attention to areas with potential obstructions, such as SMA connectors or battery contacts, and ensure they are free from debris or corrosion.

  - o Use compressed air or a soft brush to remove any dust or particles from crevices or hard-to-reach areas.

  - o For a more thorough cleaning, use a mild cleaning solution specifically designed for electronics and apply it sparingly to the cloth before wiping the surfaces.

  - o Allow the device to dry completely before reassembling or using it to avoid any moisture-related issues.

  - o Conduct regular cleaning and maintenance checks to prevent buildup or damage that could affect the device's performance or longevity.

- **Proper storage & handling:** Baofeng units should be treated as delicate measurement devices, requiring a pristine static-free environment. Avoid careless stacking that could inflict impact shears or structural stresses. Combined arms manuals cover transportation and stowage guidelines for avoiding distortion, moisture ingress, or thermal shocks outside Baofeng's rated tolerance. Spare yourself the sad sayings about malfunctions from preventable mishandling.

- **Battery care:** Half of the folks out there think rechargeable energy cells are robust Duracells to be used and discarded on a whim. No. You need to enforce a religious lifespan extension protocol for salvaging every last potential discharge cycle from our power packs. Shallow discharge practices, avoiding heat saturation, proper electrolyte maintenance—it all matters exponentially in recapturing mAh capacity and runtime longevity. Some tips include:

○ Store batteries in a cool, dry place away from direct sunlight and extreme temperatures to prevent overheating and deterioration.

○ Use high-quality batteries and chargers recommended by Baofeng to ensure compatibility and safety.

○ Regularly charge your Baofeng radio batteries according to the manufacturer's guidelines to maintain optimal performance.

○ Avoid overcharging or leaving batteries plugged in for extended periods, as this can lead to decreased battery life and potential damage.

○ Avoid exposing batteries to water or moisture, as this can damage the cells and lead to malfunctions.

○ When not in use, remove batteries from the radio to prevent drainage and extend their lifespan.

○ Monitor battery levels regularly during use and recharge as needed to avoid sudden power loss during critical operations.

○ If storing batteries for an extended period, partially charge them to around 50% capacity to prevent degradation while in storage.

○ Invest in spare batteries or portable power banks for backup power during emergencies or extended operations.

○ Follow proper disposal guidelines for old or damaged batteries to protect the environment and prevent hazardous waste.

Inspection standards, storage/handling SOPs, and energy cycle preservation: you are ingraining these preventive cleaning practices so deeply that they become second nature. Batteries, cases, buttons, knobs, terminals: each component should receive the same daily care and attention that the world's most advanced radio telescopes receive.

Recommended Accessories for Enhancing Performance and Durability

Even if you keep your radio gear in top-notch condition, there's a point where it can only do so much with its standard setup. That's why the next step is a complete system overhaul for your Baofeng gear. You'll outfit it with top-of-the-line aftermarket upgrades that turn them into high-performance Spec-Ops communication tools.

- **High-quality antennas:** Forget the bundled sad rubber whips that ship with these handsets. Upgrade to specialized antennas designed for maximum signal strength and precise radiation patterns. Look into:
  - **Directional Yagi antennas**: Yagi antennas are known for their directionality, meaning they focus their signal in a specific direction rather than broadcasting evenly in all directions. They consist of multiple elements, including a driven element and directors and reflectors. The purpose of a directional Yagi antenna is to increase signal strength and coverage in a specific direction, making it ideal for point-to-point communication or targeting distant stations.

  - **Corner reflector helical antennas**: Corner reflector antennas use a flat, reflective surface (the corner reflector) behind a radiating element to increase the antenna's directivity and gain. Helical antennas are coil-shaped and can be used for circular polarization. Combining these two designs creates a corner reflector helical antenna, which offers high gain and improved signal reception compared to standard omni-directional antennas. These antennas are often used in satellite communication and radio astronomy applications.

  - **Axial-mode helical antenna:** An axial-mode helical antenna is a type of helical antenna designed to operate in its fundamental mode of operation, known as axial mode. These antennas are characterized by a spiral structure with a central axis along which the RF current flows. Axial-mode helical antennas offer circular polarization and high gain, making them suitable for applications where robust signal strength and polarization diversity are important, such as satellite communication and space tracking systems.

- **Protective cases and holsters:** But none of those portals can work properly if the power source is damaged by field hazards. Which is why protecting your gear is crucial. Outfit each radio with tough protective cases and holsters from top brands like Pelican and Kydex. These cases are built to withstand shocks, water, and extreme conditions, ensuring your radios stay safe no matter what challenges you face in the field.

- **External mics & speakers:** For improved interaction, add external audio components to your units.

  These components deliver clear and crisp audio even in noisy environments. Look into directional modulated mic loops, high-decibel speakers with noise-canceling features, and encrypted subvocal throat relays—all aimed at ensuring flawless communication.

Miscommunications lead to dead air, which leads to dead signalmen. These enhancements transform radios into robust military-grade devices, combining the awareness of a military command center with the agility of advanced mobility suits.

Every detail should be optimized, from custom mounts to battery arrangements, ensuring your communication setup surpasses ordinary standards.

CONCLUSION

We've finished the last chapter, and now your mind should be primed for tactical expertise, impressing even the IPBCS (Integrated Personnel and Battle Command System, a military system used for coordinating personnel and command operations during battle) battle staff.

You've absorbed insights ranging from encryption methods to legal guidelines and network structures, leaving no topic unexplored. You've evolved into a skilled master of waveforms, adept at managing every frequency in the electromagnetic spectrum with precision. What once seemed cryptic now makes sense to you. However, we've only scratched the surface of this vast transmission reality. The techniques you've learned so far are just the beginning—a foundation to build upon. Put this hidden knowledge into action through practical testing and hands-on learning. Each new experience will reveal more about the intricate workings of your interconnected signal network. Dive deep into the circuits and unravel the mysteries of GETS principles. For Baofeng radios, the GETS principles can be quite handy. GETS stands for Goals, Environment, Tasks, and Skills, a framework to help users maximize their radio usage effectively.

It's crucial to note that Baofeng's ongoing innovation and focus on affordability have made advanced radio communications accessible to a wider audience.

Their product lines, especially the legendary UV-5R, have put advanced features into the hands of amateur operators at incredibly low price points compared to other manufacturers. This has opened up new horizons for communities to establish robust emergency preparedness and resilient communication networks. As you dive deeper into the programming capabilities of these radios, you'll find they pack surprising flexibility that masks their cost. The ability to customize code plugs from the ground up allows tailoring to specialized needs, from public service organizations to intricate hobbyist projects. With enough programming know-how, features like cross-band repeat functionality can be unlocked. Mesh networking has been a particular area of intense Baofeng innovation and user experimentation. Combining radios into self-healing, self-configuring mesh networks enables resilient data and voice transmission without infrastructure dependencies. Evolving protocols like MMDVM (Multi-Mode Digital Voice Modem, which is a hardware and software project designed to enable amateur radio operators to operate digital voice modes on repeaters and simplex links) are extending this decentralized communication robustness even further. Hobbyists have even begun meshing radios with technologies like LoRa (Long Range, which is a low-power, wide-area networking (LPWAN) technology designed to enable long-range communication with low power consumption) sensors for environmental monitoring.

Importantly, Baofeng's commitment to open-source software and hardware has fostered an immense knowledge-sharing community. Online forums actively discuss new techniques, share code, and troubleshoot niche issues. Many enthusiasts have published comprehensive programming guides specifically tailored to different Baofeng models and use cases. This wealth of resources empowers you to continually expand your skills. While already incredibly feature-rich, Baofeng's product pipeline shows no signs of slowing down on packing more capabilities into affordable radio platforms. Third-party developers continually enhance functionality through apps, modded firmware, and code plugins. AI voice interfaces, encrypted multimedia streaming, and advanced spectrum visualization tools could all become standard in future radios. The insights you've gained have prepared you to stay at the cutting edge as this radio technology rapidly evolves. Maintaining your edge will ensure you extract maximum utility and cutting benefit from whatever amazing radios Baofeng has in the pipeline next.

Hey, you weathered the synaptic storm. But this milestone does not mark an ending, but an inflection point for your mastery's true beginning. Your journey ahead unfolds like an infinite multiverse, filled with endless possibilities waiting to be explored. Embrace the thrilling uncertainties and paradoxes that lie ahead, savoring the sensory overload of discovery. Stay hungry for the uncharted territories of radio mastery beyond these pages.

Imagine yourself as an interconnected NEXUS, a vital part of a vast network of knowledge. All it takes is your unyielding curiosity to keep growing, learning, and connecting at an unparalleled level.

As you push past your limits, I have one request: share your thoughts through a review, capturing your journey with these invaluable resources. Your review will guide other brave adventurers eager to join our expansive and interconnected radiative community.

The call for unity beckons.

REFERENCES

alazarsemere. (2019, March 1). *How to fix four common two-way radio problems*. Tridon. https://www.tridon.com/four-common-two-way-radio-problems-and-how-to-fix-them/

arcanecode. (2019, April 11). *Programming your Baofeng radio with Chirp and solving the prolific driver issue*. Arcane Code. https://arcanecode.com/2019/04/11/programming-your-baofeng-radio-with-chirp-and-solving-the-prolific-driver-issue/

Arthur. (2023, March 19). *Walkie talkie accessories: Must-have add-ons for your communication needs*. Herda. https://herdaradio.com/blog/radio-purchase-guide/must-have-walkie-talkie-accessories/

Baofeng radios: The comprehensive guide for amateur radio operators. (2024, March 27). Mastering ham radio: From Exam Prep to General Insights. https://examwave.net/baofeng-radios-the-comprehensive-guide-for-amateur-radio-operators/

BaoFeng Tech. (n.d.). *BaoFeng compare chart*. Baofeng. https://baofengtech.com/wp-content/uploads/2020/10/CompareChart.pdf

Baofeng UV-5R manual. (n.d.). Baofengtech. Retrieved May 7, 2024, from https://baofengtech.com/wp-content/uploads/2020/09/BaoFeng_UV-5R_Manual.pdf

Baofeng walkie talkie accessories. (n.d.). Baofeng Radio. Retrieved May 7, 2024, from https://www.baofengradio.co.uk/walkie-talkies-accessories/

Black, B. (n.d.). *Ultimate radio communication guide: What to look for in a handheld transceiver*. ITS Tactical. Retrieved May 7, 2024, from https://www.itstactical.com/digicom/comms/ultimate-radio-communication-guide-what-to-look-for-in-a-handheld-transceiver/

Black, B. (2014, October 30). *The ultimate guide to learning about radio communication and why you should*. ITS Tactical. https://www.itstactical.com/digicom/comms/the-ultimate-guide-to-learning-about-radio-communication-and-why-you-should/

Catalog products. (n.d.). Baofeng. Retrieved May 6, 2024, from https://www.baofengradio.com/collections/catalog-products

Centers, J. (2020, November 16). *Must-have BaoFeng radio accessories for tactical comms, go-bags, and cars*. The Prepared. https://theprepared.com/blog/baofeng-accessories/

Centers, J. (2021, March 24). *How to manually program a BaoFeng radio*. The Prepared. https://theprepared.com/gear/guides/baofeng-radio-manual-programming/

Chen, J. (2021a, October 31). *Two way radio glossary of abbreviations & terms*. Baofeng. https://www.baofengradio.com/blogs/news/two-way-radio-glossary

Chen, J. (2021b, November 30). *The facts about distance: What's the range for radio?* Baofeng. https://www.baofengradio.com/blogs/news/the-facts-about-distance

Choosing the right ham radio: A must-read guide. (2023, December 21). Toolify.ai. https://www.toolify.ai/gpts/choosing-the-right-ham-radio-a-mustread-guide-319834

Craig. (n.d.). *Seven steps to avoid most Baofeng radio problems*. RF Gear 2 Go. Retrieved May 7, 2024, from https://www.rfgear2go.com/baofeng-hints

Dave. (2020, April 6). *How to use and program a BaoFeng radio: Guide for beginners*. Purdylounge. https://purdylounge.com/programming-a-baofeng-radio/

Diedrich, P. (2024, February 12). *Emergency communications: Baofeng and beyond*. RECOIL OFFGRID. https://www.offgridweb.com/preparation/emergency-communications-baofeng-and-beyond/

Digital, B., & Hall, J. (2024, January 19). *Proactive two-way radio maintenance and repair maximizes lifespan*. Callmc. https://callmc.com/radio-maintenance-repair-maximizes-radio-lifespan/

Draper, J. (2024, January 2). *Best handheld ham radios for survival & beginners in 2024*. SAVENETRADIO. https://www.savenetradio.org/best-handheld-ham-radio/

Ellery, J. (2012, May 2). *Radio communication procedure for security*. Security Solutions Media. https://www.securitysolutionsmedia.com/2012/05/02/radio-communication-for-security/

Enhancing your handheld radio's performance with a "Rat Tail" antenna mod. (n.d.). Baofengtech.

Gunfire - airsoft shop, airsoft guns, tactical equipment. (n.d.). Gunfire. https://gunfire.com/en/producers/baofeng-1451303147.html

ham Radio Prep. (2019, December 18). *Why you should consider a Baofeng Handheld for ham radio*. ham Radio Prep. https://hamradioprep.com/baofeng-vhf-and-uhf-handheld-radio/

Hanna, K. T. (n.d.). *What is frequency-hopping spread spectrum (FHSS)?* SearchNetworking. https://www.techtarget.com/searchnetworking/definition/frequency-hopping-spread-spectrum

Home - CHIRP. (n.d.). Chirpmyradio. Retrieved May 7, 2024, from https://chirpmyradio.com/projects/chirp/wiki/Home

Joe. (2020, May 5). *How to get your ham radio license in 3 simple steps*. ham Radio Prep. https://hamradioprep.com/how-to-get-your-ham-radio-license-made-easy/

Keeping conversations private and secure with two way radios. (n.d.). 2826. Retrieved May 7, 2024, from https://2826.co.uk/news/private-conversations-two-way-radio#:~:text=Using%20a%20private%20channel%3A%20When

KØNR, B. (2014, February 8). *Solving the Baofeng cable problem*. AmateurRadio.com. https://www.amateurradio.com/solving-the-baofeng-cable-problem/

M4D. (n.d.). *Taking care of your two-way: 7 Simple steps*. Tridon. Retrieved May 7, 2024, from https://www.tridon.com/taking-care-of-your-two-way-7-simple-steps/

M4D. (2018, June 13). *Basic jargon: Dummy's guide to radio terminology*. Tridon. https://www.tridon.com/radio-terminology-dummys-guide/

Master the basics of Baofeng UV-5R with a quick start guide. (2023, December 19). Toolify.ai. https://www.toolify.ai/gpts/master-the-basics-of-baofeng-uv5r-with-a-quick-start-guide-334865

Mclaren, S. (2023, December 10). *ham radio buyer's guide: How to choose the best ham radio*. Stryker Radios. https://strykerradios.com/ham-radios/ham-radio-buyers-guide/

Noonan, T. (n.d.-a). *BaoFeng UV-5R - Emergency communication & frequencies*. Bug out Bag Builder. https://www.bugoutbagbuilder.com/learning-tutorials/baofeng-uv-5r-basic-setup-emergency-frequencies#:~:text=To%20setup%20the%20radio%2C%20ensure

Noonan, T. (n.d.-b). *Baofeng UV-5R: Basic setup & emergency frequencies*. Bug out Bag Builder. Retrieved May 7, 2024, from https://www.bugoutbagbuilder.com/learning-tutorials/baofeng-uv-5r-basic-setup-emergency-frequencies

Option Gray. (2022, May 23). *Off-grid communications – ham radio vs. satellite phones*. Bema International. https://www.blackemergmanagersassociation.org/2022/05/emergency-communications-ham-radio-vs.html

Parecki, A. (2020, October 20). *Baofeng cheat sheet*. W7APK. https://w7apk.com/baofeng

Pujalt, C. (2023, November 10). *Maximize the lifespan of your two-way radio system*. EMCI Wireless. https://www.emciwireless.com/our-blog/maximize-the-lifespan-of-your-two-way-radio-system/

Pujalt, C. (2024, February 5). *Understanding FCC regulations for two-way radio systems*. Emci Wireless. https://www.emciwireless.com/our-blog/fcc-regulations-for-two-way-radio-systems/

Radio troubleshooting: Common problems & how to fix them. (n.d.). Air Comm. Retrieved May 7, 2024, from https://www.aircomm.com/blog/radio-troubleshooting-common-problems

Raven. (2020, March 15). *Baofeng for beginners: More on antennas, range, and emergency use (video)*. Talon Survival. https://talonsurvival.com/baofengforbeginners2/

Rick. (2016, August 10). *How to manually program the Baofeng UV-5R from the keypad.* Buy Two Way Radios. https://www.buytwowayradios.com/blog/2016/08/how_to_manually_program_the_baofeng_uv-5r_from_the_keypad.html

Step-by-Step Guide to Getting Your 10-year GMRS License: Easy application process explained. (n.d.). Baofengtech.

10-Baofeng help menu1-40 features explained. (n.d.). K7jep. https://k7jep.org/wp-content/uploads/simple-file-list/10-Baofeng-Help_Menu1-40_Features_Explained_2022-07-13_9.pdf

The lifeline when everything else fails: Baofeng radios for survival communication. (2023, October 16). Creek Stewart. https://www.creekstewart.com/creek-stewart-survival/the-lifeline-when-everything-else-fails-baofeng-radios-for-survival-communication

The Official Baofeng Store. (n.d.). Baofeng. Retrieved May 6, 2024, from https://www.baofengradio.com/?gad_source=1&gclid=CjOKCQjw_-GxBhC1ARIsADGgDjsAZCEV-6KoxyXUchXBih7MrAwl0oTAmCaJ-WdgZueKWpibL7ToET1gaAoTZEALw_wcB

The public and broadcasting. (n.d.). Federal Communications Commission. https://www.fcc.gov/media/radio/public-and-broadcasting

Thomas, T. (2023, September 5). *The basics of two-way radio encryption.* First Source Wireless. https://firstsourcewireless.com/blogs/blog/radio-encryption

Troubleshooting. (n.d.). Baofeng. https://baofeng.zendesk.com/hc/en-us/sections/360000126272-Troubleshooting

UV-82HP user manual. (n.d.). Baofengtech. https://baofengtech.com/wp-content/uploads/2020/09/UV82HP_Manual_ReducedSize.pdf

What antenna on a BaoFeng UV-5R Pro will give me better reception? (n.d.). Amateur Radio Stack Exchange. Retrieved May 7, 2024, from https://ham.stackexchange.com/questions/1469/what-antenna-on-a-baofeng-uv-5r-pro-will-give-me-better-reception

Why isn't my Baofeng FM radio working? (n.d.). Baofengtech. https://baofengtech.com/blog-why-isnt-my-baofeng-fm-radio-working/

Zhong, E. (2022, August 15). *How to program Baofeng UV-5R series with programming software.* Baofeng. https://www.baofengradio.com/blogs/news/how-to-program-baofeng-uv-5r-series-with-programming-software

IMAGE REFERENCES

AbsolutVision. (2017). [Image]. In *Unsplash*. https://unsplash.com/photos/photo-of-bulb-artwork-82TpEld0_e4

Banks, C. (2019). Five human hands on brown surface [Image]. In *Unsplash*. https://unsplash.com/photos/five-human-hands-on-brown-surface-LjqARJaJotc

Carvalho, W. (2021). [Image]. In *Pexels*. https://www.pexels.com/photo/transmission-towers-under-a-night-sky-8176752/

CQF-Avocat. (2017). [Image]. In *Pexels*. https://www.pexels.com/photo/scrabble-tiles-613508/

Das, A. (2022). [Image]. In *Pexels*. https://www.pexels.com/photo/person-holding-a-black-two-way-radio-14194761/

Dent, J. (2020). [Image]. In *Unsplash*. https://unsplash.com/photos/black-and-silver-door-knob-3wPJxh-piRw

Duong, C. (2017). Bff [Image]. In *Unsplash*. https://unsplash.com/photos/silhouette-photo-of-six-persons-on-top-of-mountain-Sj0iMtq_Z4w

Gatewood, H. (2019). [Image]. In *Unsplash*. https://unsplash.com/photos/black-and-white-usb-data-cables-QM9yzAoX-GQ

Grabowska, K. (2020a). [Image]. In *Pexels*. https://www.pexels.com/photo/cardboard-box-on-dark-wooden-table-near-tape-and-scissors-4498152/

Grabowska, K. (2020b). [Image]. In *Pexels*. https://www.pexels.com/photo/roll-of-american-dollars-tightened-with-red-band-4386471/

Huber, J. (2021). Abstract lights [Image]. In *Unsplash*. https://unsplash.com/photos/blue-and-white-light-streaks-SqR_XkrwwPk

Jodoin, M.-O. (2017). Ottawa road in the evening [Image]. In *Unsplash*. https://unsplash.com/photos/long-exposure-photography-of-road-and-cars-NqOInJ-ttqM

NASA. (2015). Photo of outer space [Image]. In *Unsplash*. https://unsplash.com/photos/photo-of-outer-space-Q1p7bh3SHj8

Nasef, O. S. (2020). Screws on black floor [Image]. In *Unsplash*. https://unsplash.com/photos/black-and-white-abstract-painting-0dy0i_je0q8

Nilov, M. (2021). [Image]. In *Pexels*. https://www.pexels.com/photo/close-up-shot-of-a-law-book-8731039/

rc.xyz NFT gallery. (2021). [Image]. In *Unsplash*. https://unsplash.com/photos/a-close-up-of-a-key-on-a-table--o90yRQoXAM

Saif71.com. (2021). Top view of four yellow AA batteries on wooden background [Image]. In *Unsplash*. https://unsplash.com/photos/yellow-plastic-hair-comb-on-black-surface-XWjWtl8B-qo

Smith, K. (2017). [Image]. In *Pexels*. https://www.pexels.com/photo/brown-bare-tree-551615/

Spiske, M. (2018). [Image]. In *Unsplash*. https://unsplash.com/photos/matrix-movie-still-iar-afB0QQw

Vazquez, H. (2023). [Image]. In *Pexels*. https://www.pexels.com/photo/man-talking-on-a-handheld-transceiver-15440100/